THE
CHURCH
AND THE
RITES
OF
PASSAGE

W. WAYNE PRICE

BROADMAN PRESS
Nashville, Tennessee

For
Jo Anna, Portia, and Jessica—
with whom I journey

© Copyright 1989 • Broadman Press
All rights reserved
4284-27

ISBN: 0-8054-8427-2
Dewey Decimal Classification: 259
Subject Heading: MINISTRY // COUNSELING
Library of Congress Catalog Number: 88-37171

Printed in the United States of America

Library of Congress Cataloging-in-Publication Data

Price, W. Wayne, 1938-
    The church and the rites of passage / W. Wayne Price.
        p.   cm.
    ISBN 0-8054-8427-2 : $3.25
        1. Occasional services—Baptists.   2. Baptists—Liturgy.
    3. Baptists—Customs and practices.   I. Title.
    BX6337.P75   1989   88-37171
    265—dc19   CIP

Contents

Introduction

On a sunny fall morning in 1956 a seventeen-year-old boy loaded two small suitcases into the trunk of a friend's car, waved to his mother and baby brother, and set out for a college two-hundred miles away. I was that young man. The only ceremony to this most important transition of my young life was a good-bye to only one fourth of my family of origin; the others were at work or school. My church, so important throughout my life, was completely uninvolved. All the emotions of such a going-away poured over me like warm water: excitement to be setting out on my own, fear of the new and of possible failure, and pride that I was the only person in my extended family, as far as I knew, who had ever gone to college. I remember feeling incredibly alone!

I was so caught up in the emotions of the experience that I had no ability to be theoretical or analytical; I figured out much later that too little was made over this transition in my life. I would also learn that I was actually passing through a gateway from one "stage" of my life to another. The process of applying to college, arranging a few financial details, setting a departure date and a mode of travel, saying good-bye to my family and leaving, were all part of a ceremony, a ritual. The process may have been informal, uncomplicated, simple, understated; it was, nevertheless, a ritual of going away and it was repeated about that same time by families all over the nation.

Rites and rituals are set, preserved, watched over, and altered by the social groups to which we belong. By their very definition, they are attended by the social group which maintains them. In the case of my going away to college, my cultural group had no defined ritual for saying good-bye. The need I felt could be filled for others who came after me if some kind of rituals could be established. In some of the other transitions—birth, marriage, and death—rituals do exist even though many of those who need such ceremonies are nowadays separated from the social groups which oversee them.

We have become a society in geographical transition, taking the moving van to distant places in quest of our fortunes. Many of us have become prosperous but, in the process, we have cut ourselves off from our roots, our support systems. Young couples frequently go through the birth process without a single family member or longtime friend present. Funerals are often conducted with only a handful of mourners. Many marriage ceremonies are performed by clergy who scarcely know the couple, and witnessed by a group with whom the couple has an unfortunately brief history.

Our culture, after several decades of separation from the rituals and the communities overseeing them, may just now be recognizing their value. We may be just now arriving at a point of understanding rituals which several decades ago we took for granted. We may just now participate in the process of taking a phrase from the academic realm and making it a part of common vocabulary: "rites of passage." We participate in these ceremonies in all our major transitions, whether or not we name them or even write them down. But our cultural uprootedness is forcing us to talk in academic terms about what we fear we are losing.

In fact, the rituals and ceremonies attached to every major transition—whether from one life stage to another or from one life situation to another—are called "rites of passage." This terminology formerly belonged to anthropology, a discipline given to the study of human beings, their origin, nature, and social relationships. Anthropologists have contributed enormously to our understanding of the essential transitions in the life cycle—usually birth, transition from childhood to adulthood, marriage, and death. Anthropologists have studied these transitions by observing the various rituals which attend them, and doing so in a variety of cultural settings. Those rituals and ceremonies—present, although different in every social structure—inform the transition, the passage.

Closely akin to anthropology and its study of the rites of passage is psychology and its concern among other issues with stages in the life-cycle. The "passages" dealt with by anthropology are somewhat expanded to include such periods as infancy; early, middle, and later childhood; adolescence; young adulthood, middle adulthood and senior adulthood. Of course the life-cycle studies include the passages of birth, marriage, and death, as well as the secondary ones. Some of these passages from one life cycle to the next occur without ritual or ceremony; others take place with the help of celebrations of varying elaboration.

Some of the rituals connected with our transitions could be classified as secular, and some as sacred; such a division, however, has been a modern distinction. Because religious practice, and for the purpose of this discussion, the church, is ever the primary guardian of both the ceremony and the content of the major transitions in our lives, the church must monitor and evaluate both the passages and the rituals which attend them. Consciously or unconsciously, religion in general and the church specifically is constantly adjusting its involvement in our stages and transitions.

Many of those within the free church tradition (since the Reformation) have tended to be suspicious of ritual and ceremony. Attempts to distance themselves from "high-church" formality often meant rejection of some rituals and ceremonies almost essential to the healthy process of passing from one life stage or situation to the next. One particular and personal experience illustrates the point.

Our first child was born in 1970. The experience was so powerful we could not have dealt with our emotions apart from the realm of the Spirit and the help of the faith community. The church we served celebrated informally with us during the weeks of expectancy. They provided the baby with a shower of gifts even before she arrived, and finally greeted her with flowers, cards, and visits. But something was lacking. My free-church tradition without christening rituals seemed to leave us hanging. We needed something not a part of our Baptist tradition. As a boy, I had attended the baptisms of my infant cousins; they were solemn but joyful times of worship. But the personal and corporate theology of my Baptist heritage rejected infant baptism, and by extension, any ceremony involving the infant's coming into the family of the church as well.

Not entirely satisfied, my wife and I in cooperation with the church created a ritual of our own. (I am now aware that some Baptist churches in 1970 practiced the dedication of babies as a part of services of worship; I knew of none at the time.) I announced our need and desire to the church, and to my delight the church responded enthusiastically. My parents purchased the baby a white dress for the occasion. My chaplain friend agreed to deliver the sermon and offer a prayer of dedication. A service of baby dedication was held, to the joy of both parents and church family. A formal ritual of passage was thereby established in that church—and a happy tradition it has become!

Four years later our second child was born and the scenario was repeated in the church to which we had subsequently moved. The ritual has become a tradition in that church as well. I take no credit for "starting something"; I simply reached out for some spiritual nurture at a time of my need and the church responded. If it had not been my need, it would have in time been the need of someone else. It may be enough to say that many have left the free church for more formal denominations because such needs were not being met. Such an exodus is no longer necessary. Larger numbers of so-called nonliturgical churches, Baptists in particular, have become increasingly sensitive to the transitions in the life cycle which demand celebrations and rituals. Ceremonies like baby dedications are now part of worship services where twenty-five years ago they would not have been possible.

Such "rites of passage" as baby dedications, baptisms, weddings, and funerals provide those involved in the transition some spiritual resources for looking back, letting go or taking hold, and moving forward.[1] They offer some sanctity for the process of looking ahead, going on. By bringing these life needs and transitions to the altar of God, resources such as prayer, the Scriptures, Christian theology, and the faith community can offer appropriate help, healing, or simply support. Nearly every transition involves grief over what is being left behind; ritual in a community context says we are allowed to grieve and we have caring people to grieve with us. Nearly every transition involves exhilaration and excitement; who can bubble over alone! Nearly every transition involves fear of the unknown. (Can I do college work? Will I be a good parent? How will I manage now that he/she is dead?) Who better than the church can stand with us at such times!

Grief and letting go, anxiety about the future, and exhilaration in the present are personal emotions and to some extent private; they are not, however, exclusive. The death of someone touches many people besides the nuclear family, and many of those people attend the funeral and enter the formal grieving process for that individual. Indeed, John Donne rightly connected private and personal grief to the larger community: the bell tolls for all of us. The community which gathers to celebrate the life and mark the death of one of its members does much more: it raises openly the issue of death for the entire congregation. The community celebrates life itself, reaffirms the goodness of life even in the face of death and celebrates a hope for life beyond life. The funeral rituals for one member of a given community belong to all the members. The same can be said of all the rites of passage of our lives. Who can witness a baptism without recalling his or her own baptism? Who can attend a wedding without recalling or fantasizing about one's own wedding? We need not be surprised to see people weep at such ceremonies, even when they are not particularly close to those involved.

All this is to notice and applaud the efforts of many churches in the free-church tradition for their attempts to celebrate ritually the transitions in our lives. Out of my own personal need and my own experience of more than thirty years as a Baptist pastor, I want to offer first of all an overview of the transitions which need rituals in worship. I have chosen birth, baptism, graduation, marriage, retirement, and death as the primary passages or transitions demanding ceremony and ritual by the church. I include a final chapter on general transition which I term, "going away." I think specifically about divorce, relocation to another community, and job/career change. Included in these observations will be some specific suggestions about the nature and content of some rituals and ceremonies I have found helpful or imagine to be worth some experimentation. I have found church members not only willing but anxious to discuss, plan, and participate in worship which includes or recognizes rites of passage. As a matter of fact, so many in my relationship have volunteered to undertake responsibility that I cannot help but conclude that people are hungry for worship that addresses their life situations. They want visual images to assist their worship and, most of all, they want to participate rather than merely watch and listen.

Professional ministers who value formal rituals of passage discover that these transition times are the most natural occasions they ever encounter for evangelism and growth in faith. The people directly involved in such changes are sensitive to faith issues and anxious for a community to guide them and interpret the events. Perhaps in this cultural period of uprootedness, the church has her best opportunity for ministry during these need times. The formal rituals allow the individuals to choose the level of their involvement and the extent to which they express their needs.

Do such emphases pose a danger that the free-church tradition might return to pre-Reformation abuse of ritual. That danger always exists. Form easily substitutes for content. Yet, we continue to use rituals. Even the ordinances of baptism and the Lord's Supper given us in the New Testament are often no more than ritual—dry, lifeless, boring, empty. Their content can only be assured by the presence of the Spirit living in the celebrants and the communicants. So once again we have this treasure in clay pots, and that need not devalue either the treasure or the vessels. Rituals of passage can and should empower the pilgrim for the journey.

Beyond the issue of abuse of ritual, we need to beware of trivializing the rituals of passage by imagining a ceremony for every single transition. As a pastor I would resist funerals for pets and the dedication of skateboards. I have much less fear of such temptations than I do of all the major celebrations we omit.

I still recall my own need time at age seventeen. I didn't know then exactly what I needed; I do now. I could have been helped immeasurably had my church on the Sunday preceding my departure gathered several of us at the altar to say with us and to us, "Fear not!" or "We are proud of you!" or "We believe in you!" or "We will support you in the following ways. . . ." I remain grateful that my Baptist family has seldom failed me, but it has not been flawless. As a pastor, I have accepted a portion of the responsibility to help the local church find ways to be present not only when the fabric is of one piece, but also in the seams.

These observations and suggestions are offered in that spirit.

Notes

1. Arnold Van Gennep, *The Rites of Passage* (Chicago: University of Chicago Press, 1960). Gennep speaks about rites of separation, transition, and incorporation. I generally follow this division but occasionally see the separation category as one of preparation.

1
Birth

"Before I formed you in the womb, I knew you." (Jer. 1:5a).

Thomas Hardy, turn-of-the-century British writer, wrote a poem entitled "The Unborn." The speaker in the poem describes a fantasy of a night visit to an imaginary womb where many, many infants await birth. They ask their visitor to describe the place into which they were soon to go. Here is the poem:

The Unborn
I rose at night, and visited
    the Cave of the Unborn:
And crowding shapes surrounded me
For tidings of the life to be,
Who long prayed the silent Head
    to haste its advent morn.

Their eyes were lit with artless trust
    Hope thrilled their every tone;
"A scene the loveliest, is it not?
A pure delight, a beauty spot
Where all is gentle, true and just,
    And darkness is unknown?"

My heart was anguished for their sake,
    I could not frame a word;

> And they descried my sunken face,
> And seemed to read therein a trace
> The news that pity would not break,
>   Nor truth leave unaverred.
>
> And as I silently retired
>   I turned and watched them still,
> And they came helter-skelter out.
> Driven forward like the rabble rout
> Into the world they so desired,
>   By the all-immanent Will.[1]

The unborn imagine a life of gentle loveliness where darkness is unknown. But the visitor turns away from them, knowing the truth: Their lives will not be ideal and their home will not be completely "true and just."

In typical Hardy fashion, the tone is fatalistic and depressing. But who can miss the truth of it? Birth often comes amid lofty expectations. Ours will be the perfect child! We will do it right! This child will mold us into a real family! In all these expectations we ignore the not-so-subtle hint of things to come—morning sickness, a difficult labor, a painful birth process. We even deny early indicators of imperfection soon after the birth—tensions of competition among mother/father/child, colic, all-night crying, fear of illness or crib death, and the struggles about mother going back to work and father failing to pull his share of the parenting load. If the baby could imagine a perfect place, parents actually preserve the fantasy by all their efforts and denials. Thomas Hardy was not completely wrong.

Infants are not born easily, nor do they come into a perfect place—although the place may not be as imperfect as Hardy believed. Nevertheless, it is into this gap between expectations and reality that the church may step to interpret and to guide. Because so many young parents are separated from their families of origin and extended families, the task of the church may be more vital than ever. The local church becomes for many of these parents a kind of surrogate extended family.

From a very practical point of view, the new parents need help with food preparation, housework, transportation, care of siblings, and companionship. From a spiritual point of view, the new parents need rituals and ceremonies which indicate that significant others outside the blood family recognize this birth as a major event. They need help interpreting the transition, letting go or adjusting memories of the past before the coming of this child, and making vows about the future with and for this child. They need to know if God is involved and how. They need spiritual counsel to help them balance the enormity of the incarnate mystery, and the reality that they are not the only couple ever to have become parents.

From a spiritual point of view, new parents need help to set priorities and commitments. Our society has been hard at work telling those now of childbearing age that they are "special," entitled, that they "can have it all."[2] We might blame the advertising media, but the real fault lies with young adults' own parents who didn't want "my child to have it as tough as I had it." We might blame the church for the slick gospel of prosperity—be a Christian and God will make you rich, successful, and happy. With such a host of cheerleaders, many of those at childbearing age, especially those from the middle classes, have bought the line that we can pursue two careers, a full social life, an active spiritual life, and have a near-perfect home and be super-parents. Such illusions lead to disillusionment!

If young parents separated from their families of origin need help with the practical side of new parenthood, they need more help with the ideological side because they have become separated from reality by a set of impossible expectations. The church, unless a part of the problem, can indeed provide some real help for these new parents. The church can offer instructive and challenging rituals around the time of the birth of the baby. Such provisions may well determine the course and direction both parents and child will follow.

The rites and ceremonies connected with birth may be formal or informal; they must be careful and consistent. But they should be provided. How thoughtfully and significantly the local church provides and performs these rites of passage will depend upon how important the church believes the tasks of parenting and the difficulties of new parents really are.

A Case for Rituals at the Passage of Birth

Almost an axiom of life: the greater the event, the more elaborate the celebration. What event is greater than birth! Prince or pauper, the infant brings hope in the promise of newness, wonder in the routines of the commonplace, and something spiritual into the mundane and the colloquial. In the television film based upon Alex Haley's, *Roots,* the birth of the main character, Kunta Kinte, underlines the enormity of the beginning of human life. The newborn's father carries the child outside the birthing hut, moments after his birth. He holds the baby over his head, facing the starlit expanse of the night sky, and says to him, "Behold, the only thing greater than yourself." Symbolic, of course! Powerful beyond words! The birth of a human being cannot be separated from the realm of the spirit; for Christians, a child is God's gift, supremely valuable and incredibly mysterious.

The church, then, demonstrates in the rituals we design and observe the value we place upon life itself. To allow a baby to come into the world, into the household of God, into a human family, without appropriate ritual of welcome is nothing less than sacrilege. To accept a child as a gift from God without adequate expressions of both gratitude and welcome is little short of arrogance. To allow even one child to be born without commitment of every available resource for her nurture and guidance is to leave to chance the very formation of the future of a culture.

In theory the church pays lip service to all this. We read about God creating the first man and woman, breathing into them the very spirit of life so that they become living personalities. In theory the church deplores convenience abortions as a sin against life itself. In theory the church stands in opposition to every evil which degrades or destroys the lives of our children. In theory the church values human life as the crowning gift of the Creator. That theory, however, deserves a level of practical implementation equal to the value we profess to place upon life itself.

Perhaps our society has come to devalue life because we have witnessed so much death by famine, war, and abortion. Names like Vietnam and Biafra have come into our living rooms, complete with pictures of death. We have become numb to death and casual about life. Perhaps in our struggle to attain more and more material things, birth sometimes seems an inconvenience, a hindrance to other goals. Perhaps because the task of child rearing in this technological and materialistic age has become so difficult and chancy, we view birth as a liability rather than as a gift to be welcomed and prized. Whatever our hesitation, the church stands as the likely trumpet of God to call our culture again and again to place value only where true value exists.

The church, therefore, can and must proclaim the value of life by our preaching and teaching, but words are not sufficient. The symbols and rituals ought also to be set in pictures before our people and the world to demonstrate that value and our commitment to those infants who embody the very image of God. What we do to express the value of life may last longer that anything we say.

Not only does the value of life call the church to celebrations of its beginnings, that gift from God, that infant life also embodies great mystery, and this mystery calls for rituals of recognition. Jesus talked to Nicodemus about being born again, the mystery whereby spiritual life comes into existence. It is as the wind blowing—we hear it and we feel it, but we have no idea where it comes from or where it goes, even with our scientific knowledge. So it is as well with physical birth. Has there ever been a mother who did not marvel at the first stirring of life within her? Has there ever been a father who held his newborn child without a tear in his eye and a lump in his throat in the face of such miracle? Has ever a doctor or a nurse delivered a baby nonchalantly? None of us is surprised by Mary's response to the angel's message, "How shall this be?" (Luke 1:34). Even those expert in the mechanics of birth bow before the presence of such mystery.

In an age of technology, research, and knowledge the church remains one of the guardians of such divine wonder. We need not explain it or explain it away. We do need to celebrate it and make promises concerning its direction.

Rituals Available to the Church and to Parents

Since the Protestant Reformation, nonliturgical churches have viewed ritual with suspicion. We have tended to place the greater value on the spontaneous side of the leadership of God's Spirit. We have avoided christening ceremonies and prescribed prayers at birth. For obvious theological reasons we have rejected infant baptism. But we have employed far more rituals than surface appearances might suggest. Some of these rituals may be called, "informal," because they are often performed spontaneously and may be carried out by lay people.

The traditional baby shower is a ritual which may or may not be directly "spiritual" and offered by the household of faith. It is, nevertheless, a ritual which recognizes the joy of the parents and the investment of the community. Such a "party" becomes the first symbolic statement that society has a stake in the birth of a baby. This child will be given the opportunity to perpetuate the race, to carry forth our values, to accept the stewardship of life. The future of the world depends upon how responsible this child will be; the level of that responsibility depends somewhat upon the involvement of the larger community. The baby shower is far more than friendship and gifts, as important as these are to all new parents.

Prior to the birth of our first child, the church we served gave us a baby shower. We felt deeply that the entire church wanted to be a part of our excitement, and accept some of the responsibility. The generosity of the people proved almost embarrassing to the point that no new parents could have felt more completely the support of a very large group. Several days after the shower, one of the middle-aged ladies came to me with a cautious offer. She would give us her baby bed, over fifty years old and never used after she outgrew it. She was careful to allow us to refuse the gift. I immediately sensed that more was involved than getting rid of an old piece of furniture or helping the young preacher. She was carefully selecting and passing on something of herself to someone she wanted to have it.

I accepted the offer, took the bed to the basement, and scraped away enough finish to realize the wood was a very high-quality maple. I invested more than one-hundred hours in its new finish. The slow work time enabled me to grasp more fully how one generation invests in the next. This informal act of transferring a piece of baby furniture from one family to another was no less a rite of passage than the prayer of a pastor at the birth of the baby.

If a baby bed and a baby shower are informal preparatory rites of passage, others occur spontaneously around the birth time. These again are quiet but valuable expressions of concern and investment of a larger circle of friends: care of older children during the birth process, housekeeping chores, food preparation, and infant care to allow the mother some respite. One theologian called this "casserole theology"—the expression of love and concern by quiet assistance when it is most needed. We tend not to see them as rituals, but those who have benefitted from them know the spiritual power they contain.

But what about the formal rites of passage at birth? What does the church do in this transition for each newborn in the congregation? These begin with the pastor, either in the hospital or the home, as soon after birth as possible. Because the trend is toward very brief hospital stays, the mother and child may be home before the pastor receives news of the birth. This initial contact is made much easier if the pastor has been in touch with the couple during the pregnancy. The couple will sometimes say, "I want you to come see us in the hospital." Or the minister can offer them such a visit if they will call as soon as the baby is born.

This kind of advance communication enables a more effective ministry in the event of a miscarriage, a still-birth, or a birth defect. Such early involvement also enables more substantive discussion about the spiritual dimensions of parenting when the baby arrives.

The first pastoral visit is a ritual of great significance, both for its symbolic value and its content. The minister's presence says that this birth has spiritual implications, that the church stands by to interpret them, and that the church wants to enter the joy of the gift from God. Ideally, the pastor would like both parents to be present at such a visit. The conversation need not be specific in these terms, but a pastoral prayer of Thanksgiving certainly ought to incorporate all these elements.

One pastor presents a Dutch "cradle cross" at such visits. The little wooden cross is five inches high, and two-and-a-half inches across. A small eye hook on the top allows it to be hung on the wall. With the cross comes an explanation:

> But Jesus said, "Suffer little children, and forbid them not, to come unto me: for of such is the kingdom of heaven" (Matt. 19:14). The Dutch believed in this passage and for centuries placed cradle crosses over the beds of their infant children that this symbol might early become part of the child's consciousness.[3]

Each pastor will take an approach personally chosen and carefully followed. Uniformity among ministers should be less a matter of methodology and more a matter of involvement. New parents are usually honored by a pastoral visit and perhaps never more receptive to ministry.

Another of the formal rites of passage involves the people from the preschool ministries of the church, most of the time laypeople. Many churches plan a visit to the home within days of the arrival of the baby to present a small, white New Testament and a cradle-roll enrollment certificate. Again, this ritual, repeated with every child connected with the church, provides a powerful statement of parental responsibility to "bring up a child in the way he is to go" in the hope that "when he is old he will not depart from it." This visit also suggests by implication that this baby will find welcoming arms and caring hands when she comes to church.

I enjoy a quick visit to the preschool area when I happen to be in an unfamiliar church for some kind of meeting. I can get a sense of the seriousness with which a particular church approaches birth and infancy by what I see of the setting. I can always imagine how parents feel when they take their babies to those areas—and whether they will choose to return. I recall one nursery area which had a large picture poster on the wall, child's eye level, with Polaroid photographs of each child at three- or four-month intervals. The little ones and their parents could see in their church setting the growth of their children. And each three or four months at this age brings dramatic changes!

Two additional formal rituals deserve mention. First, if the church publishes a newsletter, a brief announcement of the birth enables church members to know about the birth and acknowledge it with a card or a gift. Second, a rose on the altar table and an announcement in the worship bulletin further marks the event. In some congregations, one particular family may want to see to it that a rose is on the altar table on the Sunday following the newsletter announcement. If no one from the baby's family is present in worship on that morning, a church-member friend can deliver the rose and a copy of the worship bulletin. Both rituals further involve the faith community in the birth event.

The most important of the formal rituals is the service of baby dedication. Some churches refer to it as a parent-child dedication service. This ritual can use an entire worship service with Scripture lessons, prayers, music, and sermon designed around a central theme or it can be a brief inclusion in any regular worship service. All but very large churches will probably celebrate the dedication of babies only one or two times each year because of the number of births.

For many years I have designated the Sundays between Mother's Day and Father's Day for some worship emphasis upon the home and the family. Series of sermons dealing with such themes as the marriage vows, the stages of faith development, families in the Bible, and discipleship in the home, all provide specific inspiration and assistance to families. In this context, either on Mother's Day or Father's Day, a service of baby dedication can begin or end the series with a tremendous impact upon the entire congregation.

The events following the birth of Jesus have always carried deep significance for me. We cannot imagine a couple under any more pressure than Mary and Joseph: birth to a young girl, birth away from extended family, birth in a stable, birth under threat of a maniac ruler. Yet, this couple made their way from Bethlehem to Jerusalem, ten or twelve miles, eight days after the birth, to observe all the rituals of their faith. The child was circumcised and dedicated to God; the mother underwent purification rites according to the laws of her faith. What a model for contemporary parents and the church!

Certainly, churches in the "free-church tradition" who dedicate babies make no faith decision for them. That decision to follow Christ, however, is being anticipated. Such parents promise to make available to these children all the spiritual resources necessary to help them make an informed but personal profession of faith later in life. The congregation says in such a service that they accept the responsibility to provide support for the parents and offer an environment of wisdom and nurture for the children. Although we recognize the personal nature of a profession of faith and the role of God's Spirit to call our children to faith, nevertheless, we accept some of the responsibility. In a baby dedication service, we are asking the parents to say as much for this particular child; we ask the congregation to reaffirm what they have already said for other babies in other such services. If the pastor's visit to the hospital or home was a kind of pastoral blessing, the baby dedication service is a congregational blessing.

Each pastor and congregation will by experimentation and study, and by listening to one another, arrive at some ritual which seems to fit them and the style of their particular worship. I enjoy asking fellow ministers to share with me some of the rituals they use in these passage times. Some are simple and almost spontaneous in approach; others are carefully planned. But I am impressed that those who celebrate the birth of babies in a worship service always light up when they relate their experiences.

I was understandably anxious when I exchanged pulpits with a British pastor in 1986 to inquire about their rituals in the birth passage. The pastor with whom I exchanged pulpits includes the baby and family in a regular service as soon after birth as possible. He explained how, within that service, he takes a few minutes to call the family to the altar where he talks informally to them and to the congregation about their responsibilities. While he addresses the congregation, he holds the baby in his own arms and walks up and down the aisle. At an appropriate moment, he hands the baby to an unsuspecting member of the church, thus symbolizing that the people have taken some responsibility for the child.

Not every pastor could do such a thing well, nor feel comfortable doing so. I only tell the story to illustrate the need to be creative within the context of the local church and its style. For those in search of a less spontaneous model, I offer a summary of the service I have designed and find best for the congregation I serve.

I am fortunate enough to have the resources to plan the entire service of worship around this one theme, drawing upon a wide range of music which includes organ music, hymns, children's choirs, and lay worship leaders. I always choose to preach a sermon about the family, the home, or parenting on this Sunday. The actual "Dedication for Parents and Children" is intentionally placed toward the end of the service so the congregation can greet the families at the conclusion of worship.

During the invitation hymn, which we term the "Hymn of Response," the parents go to the nursery for their children and bring them to the altar area of the sanctuary. Their names (parents and child) are on name tags which they wear. I address the parents in an informal manner on some theme of the rewards and demands of being parents. I then ask them and the congregation to join me in a responsive "covenant." The parents have seen the covenant in a prior conversation with me so I am sure they understand and agree to its contents. The covenant is as follows:

> *Minister to Parents:* Do you desire that your child shall grow up in the "nurture and admonition of the Lord," and do you as husband and wife covenant together to offer your child through the Scriptures and principles of faith a loving and obedient reverence for God and his Son, Jesus Christ?
>
> *Parents:* We do.
>
> *Minister to Parents:* And do you dedicate yourselves to Christ and His church, to live in such a way as to commend the Lord to your child always?
>
> *Parents:* We do.
>
> *Minister to Congregation:* Do you, the people of God in this place, covenant with these parents and children that you will offer love and concern for them as families, and seek to provide a community of learning, encouragement, and support in the development of their lives of faith?
>
> *Congregation:* We do.
>
> *Minister:* Having heard these statements of your desire and intent, I solemnly and joyfully commend you all to the care and protection of our Heavenly Father. I pray

the love of God and the care of the church always to be
upon (names of the babies).
Prayer of Dedication (*in unison*): We thank thee, Lord,
for the gift of these precious little ones. We gladly accept
the joyful responsibility for their growth and nurture of
body, mind, and spirit. We acknowledge them to be ours
to guide, but not to own; we accept that in our tasks we
will always be less than perfect. Allow us then the gift
of goodwill and the comfort of thy Spirit as we offer our
best to these whom thou dost love, through Jesus Christ.
Amen.

At this point a rose is presented to each family to mark the
occasion. A certificate of dedication is also prepared in advance and presented at this time.

Not every congregation will want to devote an entire service to the dedication of babies, or even do so in such a
formal manner. At the least, however, a prayer at the conclusion of a worship service, provided it is well done, can say
a great deal to the parents of a new baby.

However a dedication of parents and children is done, the
consciousness of everyone involved is raised to new heights.
They are made aware that no two parents can give their
children everything they need. Very early most parents realize their knowledge, wisdom, energy, and time are such that
many of the lessons and models the children will need must
come from extended family and surrogate family. If this has
always been true in every human culture, it seems to be more
true in this age of fast-moving technology, two-career parents, and culturally dislocated families.

I have been keenly aware that during times of family
emphasis in the church, and especially services of dedication
of parents and children, not all members of the congregation
can enter the celebrations joyfully. Some have wanted children but have been unable to bear them. Some have ex-

perienced enormous losses and failures of their children. And
some who have never married, or who divorced without
custody of their children, find such emphases in the church
agonizing.

I have little wisdom at this point, except to say that a
pastor who understands the depth of this kind of pain, and
demonstrates compassion for these members will win a place
in their hearts. In some cases, such people as these can be led
gently into the role of surrogate aunt/uncle and contribute
much to many children. Every preschool department has
someone who, although childless, devotes inordinate energy
and compassion to the children of other people. As is so often
the case, those whose pain is most intense sometimes become
the very people whose compassion for others turns out to be
the deepest. They become, in the words of the prophet Isaiah,
the suffering servants.

Every pastor who looks intently at a single area of ministry
can easily become overwhelmed. It certainly can appear such
that every age group and need area, extrapolated throughout
the congregation, would add to an already overloaded
schedule. I am keenly aware of such pressures. Yet, I find
that through such carefully planned and conducted rituals,
the minister can involve many lay people who welcome the
opportunity to be involved in the informal rituals. Further,
I have discovered that once a pattern of the ritual is in place,
the actual ceremonies require little additional time.

Ceremonies and rituals connected with birth and family
open the doors of the church to people who have been away
a long time—and to some who have never been very close.
How many ministers have stories about couples whose weddings they celebrated, who much later call to announce a
birth, and who soon after find their way into the church
family! When young people get a driver's license and a job,
they tend to leave the church; they reappear briefly to get
married, but they often come back to stay when their first

child is born. The care and seriousness with which the church welcomes babies and their parents sets the tone for the care and seriousness with which the church offers a deepening faith in Christ. Years later, the visual images of young parents standing at the sanctuary altar, holding a tiny bundle of life, outlast the pain and the difficulty of the long and arduous parenting task. One of my mind's most powerful images is that of the dedication dress my father purchased for the dedication of our first child. My father was not an overtly religious man, nor have the Baptist churches I know been excessively formal. Yet the images sharpen into focus when I think of the birth of my children have been placed there by a dress and a ceremony.

Jesus' was taken by His parents to the Temple in Jerusalem when He was eight days old. We find Him there again when He was twelve. We must assume that Mary and Joseph made at least one pilgrimage to the Temple each year. In between, Jesus must have been deeply involved in His local synagogue. Should we be surprised then that He "increased in wisdom and in stature, and in favor with God and man"! (Luke 3:52).

We return to Thomas Hardy's poem, aware that the unborn face a world less than "true and just." The degree to which the church celebrates the human passage into being will say a great deal about the kind of world those babies find.

Notes

1. Thomas Hardy, "The Unborn," *Chief Modern Poets of England and America,* Ed. Gerard DeWitt Sanders, John Herbert Nelson and M.L. Rosenthal (New York: The Macmillan Company, 1964), n.p.11.

2. Susan Littwin, *The Postponed Generation* (New York: Morrow, 1986).

3. Wallace M. Alston, Jr., "The Two Natures of the Church," Lecture II, July 2, 1986, Princeton Institute of Theology.

2
Baptism

"I am baptized!"

—Martin Luther

For many expressions of the church, baptism is bound up in birth and in naming. In fact, "christening" means giving the infant a "Christian" name—the first name. Consequently, the birth rituals include several ceremonies tied to the church. The church, so much indebted to Hebrew culture, has simply followed a pattern like that of Jesus' parents when He was born: going to the Temple; purification of the mother; circumcision of the child; presenting the child to God. Those traditions of Christianity which baptize infants largely follow these several ceremonies in pattern.

The "free-church" tradition which practices a much later baptism uses the symbols of birth but separates the rituals by a distance of years from physical birth. The period between birth and baptism in such churches may be as few as eight years, or as many as thirteen. The average age tends to be about ten to twelve years, although in recent years a startling trend has been toward much earlier baptisms. The upper end of the age ladder has no limit except death itself.

The period between birth and baptism for such churches tends to be a nurturing time. The children discover the warmth and caring of the faith community—which they associate with God—and they learn the rudiments of that faith. These include the stories from the biblical traditions, the disciplines of prayer and devotion, some sense of God and the importance of worship, and gradually their own responsibility to God and to the created order.

The period through early childhood is itself a celebrative period of discovery and joy in the love and care of God and the church. This stage of life is also a time of preparation for greater responsibility and some independent decision making. One of these decisions has to do with accepting responsibility for one's thoughts, words, and actions. In this light the child comes to a sense of the One to whom all people are ultimately responsible. Out of that sense of personal value and responsibility, the child can emerge with an even greater awareness of a love which transcends all irresponsibility, error, bad judgment, willful rebellion, and sin. That love is God's love, and it demands some specific response (ability) and commitment.

The church has given many names to this period, point, time of awareness and decision; most life-long Baptists grew up hearing it called "the age of accountability." The evangelists have spoken about it being a season of the "conviction of the Holy Spirit"—and so in a variety of expressions it is. But the awakened sense of responsibility to God, to the created order, to other people and even to oneself never comes to an end. This is merely the time of its beginning, or at least of its intensification. Nor is this period limited to the childhood years; what is awakened but not acknowledged and dealt with in these formative times continues to cry out for resolution even into adulthood. Many adults, therefore, experience much later in life what the children find much earlier. The difference may be the level of the error, bad judgment, rebellion, and sin—as well as the verbal skills to

articulate it all, and the emotional depth to feel the experience more intensely.

The later childhood years bring to the faith decision all the
sensibilities necessary to make a *life* commitment to God.
(And this is not ignore the legitimate concerns that no child,
age ten to twelve years, is wise enough, capable enough, or
experienced enough to make any *lifetime* commitments.) A
number of fine students of faith development teach us that
these children have made substantial progress in moving
away from the complete protection of nuclear and extended
families and have begun to relate confidently to a larger
human family and created order, even if these sometimes
seem impersonal or even hostile.

Those same children have developed a sense of deep and
abiding friendships. One student of human development
called this the "chumship" period.[1] These are the years of a
best friend, of unselfish and often sacrificial giving and
sharing, of telling and keeping secrets, and cooperative explorations into a broader world of nature, thought, and feeling. Parents know the time of closing and locking doors to
their rooms, building tree houses, forming clubs, needing
privacy. These kinds of youthful commitments often grow
into relationships which last a lifetime. Even the fact that
ours is a mobile society and children are often separated from
their friends of this period seems not to erase commitments.
My own daughters have friends from their preschools with
whom they maintain enviably committed relationships. I
frequently solemnize marriages in which friends who are
members of the wedding party go all the way back to early
childhood. This is a period of deep friendships and serious
commitments.

These years also boast an intellectual development capable
of understanding abstractions. Children this age, on the average, have attained a reading ability to match their powers of

memorization. (Remember the children's books so familiar to preschoolers that the parent could not skip a single word!) Now the older children are able to read and memorize, thus providing them the raw material to begin to ask theoretical questions with or without adult help. With imagination very much in place and the faith stories ever present, these children begin to face God-questions. Yet they seem to have little difficulty with Spirit-God, able to hear, love, judge—to be best friend! These developmental dynamics explain why Bibles are presented to children around this time of their lives; they further explain the reason so many children make their public professions of faith in Jesus Christ during these years.

The time is right, then, to step into a deeper level in the faith community. Much more is involved than "membership in a local church," although some specific identification and accountability structure is important. What these young people enter is, in reality, the family of God, as adopted sons/daughters of God, not by physical birth, but by spiritual birth. Indeed, the Lord Himself reminded Nicodemus that what is flesh (water/physical birth?) is flesh and what is spirit (spiritual birth?) is spirit. The kingdom of God requires both. Mystery? Yes, but a child of ten or twelve years has less difficulty with mystery than those of us who have grown too completely practical.

Studies in childhood development, then, seem to validate this age as a *kairos*—God's time—for a faith commitment. With the child standing at a distance, looking at the doorway to a deeper, long-term faith commitment, the rituals attendant upon this passage are in the hands of the church. Just as the rituals attendant upon birth in part indicate the kind of world the babies will find, so the rituals attendant upon the new birth carry enormous weight for the kind of kingdom of God the child will experience.

Rituals of Preparation

I know of no pastor or church I respect who does not prepare carefully for the baptism of children. (I am dealing only with children here because the overwhelming majority of baptismal candidates in the free-church tradition are children. Many of the same observations and even preparations are applicable to adult candidates, but modified according to age and experience.) Practically every church and every minister has developed preparation rituals over the course of many years. Surely they all bear in common a sense of the importance of the experience and profession of one's faith. The rituals grow out of individual and corporate experience.

The rituals with which I am most at home have evolved from my own experiences of what is both effective and significant; they are also the result of what I have learned from the traditions of the churches I have served, the mentors I have followed, and the books I have read. But the commitment I have to rituals of preparation for baptism, like many commitments, comes from what I needed and did not receive during my own childhood, especially at my baptism.

I grew up in a rather large Baptist church: more than one thousand members and over five hundred people every Sunday in Bible study and worship. I would consider my church to have been enlightened and progressive, orderly in all things, warmhearted, conservative in theology and worship. I grew up attending everything: Sunday School, what was called then on Sunday evening "BTU" (Baptist Training Union), two worship services every Sunday, midweek prayer meeting, and a boys' mission group. I was one of those who answered all the questions, volunteered for every part, job, or "opportunity." I knew the answers, but in retrospect, God was still for me a Bible Santa Claus—real but somehow real in the world of the imagination rather than a Spirit being.

But on a Sunday morning like most other Sunday mornings, I was jerked up short by a sensation completely new to me.

I had graduated from my mother's side near the front of the sanctuary to the back row, far corner with my friends. Even the long service was tolerable without my mother's fingers one-knuckle deep in my knee—her way of seeing to it that I "paid attention." All I really paid attention to was my knee! From my new vantage point (disadvantage point?) in the back of the sanctuary, I could sing the hymns I loved and ignore the sermons which seemed interminable. And I did. Until that fateful February Sunday on which the service was lengthened by the Lord's Supper! The routine was broken for me that day. The last hymn was being sung, and the minister was occupying his place below the pulpit and before the Communion table. Without warning or explanation I was overwhelmed with a pit-of-the-stomach awareness of a personal God. The next thing I knew, I was midway in the side aisle, headed for the pastor. He asked me if I had come to accept Jesus as my Savior, and I dutifully nodded in the affirmative. In fact, I was uncertain why I was there at all. I was "presented" to the congregation as a "candidate for baptism" and later baptized without any explanation or preparation.

Only much later in my life was I able to verbalize what was happening to me. To this day I have a deep sense that it was at this juncture of my life that I became wonderfully aware that this Jesus of the stories was alive and knew my name. Aside from all the theological explanations of sin, faith, and salvation, my conversion was for Jesus to know me and for me to say a symbolic, *yes!* That gathered congregation took me at my word/act, and accepted my spontaneous—very spontaneous—profession of faith.

Years later as a young pastor welcoming little ones like I had once been, I determined that I would baptize no one, especially a child, without the best and most detailed preparation of which I was capable. Because the ritual of baptism is itself so wonderful, it deserves some kind of preparation ritual which would help candidates understand and appreciate it to the fullness of their ability. Such preparation can and does take many forms, but I want to detail two methods I know best.

My earliest method of preparation was to schedule a conference with the child and her family. I wanted the parents to be present because they would be the ones in the first line of questions when the pastor or Sunday school teacher was not immediately available. I took a copy of a modern translation of the Bible which I used in the conference and then presented to the child. I talked very simply about sin as self-will, about God's love, about God as Friend-Savior-Lord, about a growing relationship. I wrote some of these things for the children, marked verses in their new Bibles, and even helped them verbalize a prayer of faith.

On the date of the baptism itself, I met with the child to explain the ritual of baptism itself, and some days after the baptism met with the group of those who had been baptized to talk about living and growing in faith. I always found the parents of the children grateful for the explanations. Privately, I knew some of them were hearing some of this for the first time. Like myself, many of them had been baptized years before without any word of help. Some who had never made a profession of their own faith welcomed this introduction.

In more recent years, I have changed and expanded my rituals of preparation. I have now gone to instruction classes, which seem to work well for many pastors and churches. The classes themselves number about five and last for no more than one hour and a half each. These sessions must be broken down and divided into short segments because of a child's attention span. The theme is "God as Friend." I use work

sheets with Scripture about the friendship of God, questions
about the growth of friendship, the potential barriers to
friendship, and friendship which becomes love. I have tried
to avoid the assumption that because children participate in
the classes, they will automatically decide to be baptized. I
want to leave the decision to the child, if a profession of faith
has not been made public before the classes.

The instruction classes also include discussions about worship, the architecture and arrangement of the sanctuary, and
some comparisons with other Christian traditions. Some of
these children have friends who have been sprinkled as infants and confirmed later. Some have even attended their
friends' confirmations and first Communions. These comparisons make more real and significant their own decisions.

I recall a colleague's story about a child who made a
profession of faith in a worship service. The pastor arranged
a visit in the home to discuss the situation with the parents
who were not Baptists. The parents had difficulty understanding why the boy wanted to be baptized by immersion,
inasmuch as he had been sprinkled as an infant. The young-
ster told his parents, "That baptism was for you; this one is
for me." Children sometimes understand more than adults
credit them with knowing.

In addition to the didactic part of instruction classes and
an effort to set baptism in a context of worship, some practical attention to the operations of the institutional church is
also important. My own classes pay some attention to the
function of the various church officers, the source and use of
money (and what that money symbolizes!), and how the
church governs itself. The children are more than capable of
understanding the church in ministry to its own people, and
in ministry to the world outside. All of this becomes very
personal when the youngsters see themself as an active part

of it all. This is also a good time to discuss the history and traditions of the denomination.

Each church over a period of years will see these preparation rituals develop and change. Exactly what is done and how it is done seem less important than the fact that baptism is taken so seriously by the church that careful preparations are mandatory. The children receive the unwritten, unspoken message that they are important and that baptism is one of the most important rituals in their lives.

The Ritual of Baptism

Surely, no ritual in the church, not even a funeral, involves a congregation's emotions like baptism. In traditions which practice immersion of accountable candidates, baptismal services become reenactments for nearly every person present; the few who have not been baptized by immersion seem to stand on emotional tiptoe with all sorts of questions. Each of us has his/her own story about "my baptism." I have mine.

My church was in the process of remodeling the sanctuary, so worship was held in the social hall where the congregation had met years before while the sanctuary was being built. The old baptistry had never been removed so it was pressed into service once again. On the occasion of my baptism—at the moment of my baptism, in fact—the bottom step, on which little guys like myself stood so as to be seen, *broke!* But for the preacher's sure hands and quick reflexes, the ritual would have been a true rescue. Yet two things stand out about my baptism—besides the setting and the broken step. First, my baptism was not an initiation into the Christian faith, but an expected next step in a pilgrimage begun for me years earlier, and second, some miracle and mystery were indeed hallmarks of my baptism. In spite of the broken step, and what seems always to be the Baptist sense that baptism is "just a symbol," I was much taken by the Spirit of the Lord in that ritual. It was for me a true rite of passage beyond my full understanding, even to this day.

The ritual of baptism, like all rituals, means different things to each person and carries a variety of emotional and intellectual experience levels. The church and her ministers cannot program the thoughts and feeling of the communicants, nor should we; careful preparation and sensitive administration enables each person to respond with maximum involvement of both heart and mind.

I enjoy listening to pastors talk about how they do baptisms. They seem to light up, sit forward, and speak with more intensity than usual. They always want to talk about how they have done baptisms, complete with a story about one particular experience which stands out above the others. One pastor related to a group how he had entered the sanctuary in his white baptismal robe; the candidates for baptism that evening sat on the front pew, also dressed for baptism. The hymns and lessons were carefully chosen for the candidates and the congregation, as was his short sermon. After this kind of preparation, the pastor and those to be baptized left the sanctuary and entered the baptistry by turns to celebrate the ritual they had prepared for. This pastor had laid careful plans, designed to involve everybody, prepare everybody, and create a powerful and memorable ritual. It was done dramatically, yet, without theatrics. This pastor was obviously proud of the service he had designed and conducted.

Every minister will profit from the experiences of colleagues and sister churches. Every church will be enriched by the years of experience and the willingness of a pastor to search for the fullest expression of baptism in the rituals themselves. After more than thirty years as a pastor, I have found a comfortable and beautiful ritual for baptisms, but I want to believe I am open and searching for anything that will make it more beautiful and significant.

When I came to my present assignment, one of the first requests I heard related to baptismal services was that I keep the "candle ceremony." I have been blessed by the presence of the former pastor, retired and now emeritus. I sought him out, asked him to explain the service he had used, and enlisted his participation in the first baptismal service I did in this church. I maintained nearly all his procedures and incorporated a few of my own.

Two details of this service may be informative for any baptismal service. First, I almost always include the Lord's Supper as a part of the baptismal service so that these candidates can also be recognized as receiving their initial Communion. Second, I try to allow the Scriptures, hymns, and prayers to carry the weight of communication; there is seldom a sermon in such a service.

The worship service begins in the customary preparatory ways: musical prelude, call to worship, prayer of invocation, and hymn of praise. The candidates and I wait just off the sanctuary, discussing again the meaning of the symbol, our responsibilities during the baptism, and shared prayer.

Following the opening portion of the service, a worship leader reads the first lesson from Scripture, and then the comments of Jesus about Himself as the Light of the world. The ledge in front of the baptistry is set with a series of candles: a "Christ candle," taller than the rest, which I light as the "Light of the world" text is read, and one candle for each candidate. The first candidate enters the water. I ask, "Do you (full name) confess that Jesus Christ is Lord?" and the candidate responds, "I confess that Jesus Christ is my Lord." The candidate then takes from the series of candles the one with his/her name on it, lights it from the Christ candle and replaces it. I then baptize that person. The scenario is repeated with each candidate. One candle remains on the ledge, off to the side; I or the worship leader explain that one candle remains unlit, as a reminder of all those yet to believe for whom the church bears responsibility for witness.

Those baptized enter the sanctuary, sit as a group, and at the time of the Lord's Supper, are served before the rest of the congregation. This calls attention to their first Communion. Following Communion, they are called to the area in the front center and presented with several symbols of the ritual. They are given a certificate of baptism, a wooden cross on a leather cord (placed around their necks), and are encouraged to keep their communion glasses. They are later given their baptismal candles.

How do the candidates, especially the children, respond to the ritual(s)? I know best my own daughters' responses, but I also hear from other parents. Most of the children display prominently in their homes their Communion cup, the wooden cross, and the candle. They become visible and continuing symbols of a rite of their passage into a deeper level of faith. The "artifacts" of the rituals remind them that something happened in their lives and on one particular day in one particular worship service, the entire congregation recognized its importance and their importance.

For each member of the congregation itself, the baptismal service is a spiritual return to some baptistry, river, creek, or lake; it is a pilgrimage of the heart to some white-framed rural church building or some large, urban sanctuary. For each member of the congregation, the baptismal service is a spiritual reminder of promises made and a journey begun. The symbol becomes immeasureably more powerful than any words. And the Communion of the Lord's Supper becomes an opportunity for rededication to the journey and the promises.

The rituals I use have been assembled from many sources

over many years. None of them are mine, nor are they the property of some pastor or congregation from whom I have borrowed them as a complete package. Rather, they have gradually shaped themselves together into forms which seem to express one particular congregation and by turns speak to that congregation. The people in our church have become wedded to the ceremony of the candles, but remarkably open to changes in nearly everything else. The point for any church is not so much to adopt and adapt the rituals of another church, as much as it is to develop rituals from many sources into traditions both meaningful and significant.

Unfortunately, most pastors seldom witness the rituals of baptism in other churches because they are seldom visiting in churches when baptism is celebrated. However, conventions, workshops, conferences, and associations of ministers afford occasions to ask several people, "Tell me how your church does baptisms." The "free-church" tradition is wonderfully open to innovation and creativity in the rituals associated with baptism.

Passage into Responsibility

If baptism in the free-church tradition is reserved for candidates who have reached some level of accountability, then some observable expressions of responsibility need to be built into the "passage." The new Christian convert—child of God—having passed through the doorway to the household of faith is expected to reflect that new life. For adults, the specifics of those responsibilities can be identified in the disciplines of faith and the tasks within the institutional church. Adults can participate in the committee process of the church, control their own devotional life and spiritual growth, and choose numerous directions which express their newfound lives of faith. Most congregations work hard at the task of making such opportunities available to adults who are baptized. More difficult is the task of finding such structures for children.

We explain to children aged ten to twelve that they are full members of the church and entitled to all the privileges and responsibilities of membership. We do not encourage them, however, to vote in business meetings, nor do we nominate them to serve on committees. We teach them the importance of financial stewardship, even giving them church offering envelopes and pledge cards, but we do not build our budgets around their contributions. Obviously, we know that baptism is a passage from some state or condition to another, but we find it difficult to set the conditions of responsibility on the other side of the passage.

Again, all churches would serve their newly baptized youngsters well by exploring avenues of responsibilities for them. I offer from my own setting some examples of how one church has attempted to address the issue. Children who are baptized are given opportunity to become "junior ushers." (They enjoy the role until about the eighth grade, and most of them take it seriously until the ninth grade.)

Our church has a long-standing tradition of burning two candles on the altar table in each service—suggesting both the humanity and divinity of Jesus. During the weeks before Christmas, we light the candles of the Advent wreath as part of our preparation for the coming of Christ. At other times of the church year additional use is made of candles. One responsibility of junior ushers is the lighting of these candles. Two young people are on the schedule each week. They wear white choir robes and sit in places reserved for them in the sanctuary. The two who serve on Communion Sunday come to the table at the appropriate time to help the pastor uncover the Communion elements; they return following Communion to cover them. The names of the two serving on a given week are printed in the weekly newsletter, giving them some recognition and underscoring the level of responsibility they have been given. Years later, children who have served in this capacity recall with pride the role they played in worship.

When these children reach the ninth grade, and sometimes before, they begin to see themselves as too grown-up for the duties of the junior ushers. Those who are willing, are appointed to be ushers, usually assigned to the fifth Sundays, under the supervision of an adult. Such are the efforts of one particular church.

Certainly, every church must provide instruction and encouragement in the disciplines of the faith life for all we baptize. We must also encourage each one in the faith life outside the meetings of the local church. And while the kinds of responsibilities open to children within the church are limited, there are a few. The best ones are created or chosen to demonstrate that when we are baptized, we are recipients of a particular grace; we have also accepted a particular level of faith responsibility. Just as baptism symbolizes a deeper level of life, so does some office like junior usher symbolize a deeper level of responsibility. I believe the children look forward to this and my experience suggests they take it quite seriously.

A Concluding Observation

Baptism which occurs during the ten-to-twelve year period is a ritual of the spirit, a rite of faith. It cannot be separated, however, from its connection with the passage from childhood to adolescence. These are years of puberty, the awakening of issues of authority, sexuality, career choices, and ultimately, identity. In recent years, the church's best students of Christian education and faith development have attended in detail to these issues as part of the larger task of the church. Puberty and adolescence issues need to be increasingly prominent in rituals associated with baptism. After all is said and done, identity, power, and sexuality deserve the light which Jesus Christ can bring to the young people who must fashion their emerging lives.

Notes

1. Wayne E. Oates, *On Becoming Children of God,* (Philadelphia: Westminster Press, 1969). pp 79*ff.* Dr. Oates has taken the term, "chumship" from Harry Stack Sullivan and elaborated upon it impressively.

3
Graduation

"In favor with God and man" (Luke 2:52).

Those over fifty years of age remember the events surrounding the coming of age. High-school graduation marked a turning point. Parents often went to great lengths to honor their youngsters who were about to embark upon adulthood and independence: invitations, a new suit or dress, a graduation party, and endless discussions about what lay ahead. For a few, college stood on the horizon; for others, it was the military; for most a full-time job and dreams of money and a car and maybe even marriage. Being "out on my own" meant independent living, decision making, responsibility, and, most of all, *freedom.*

On the day I drove away to college, I knew I had left home. I expected to return briefly, maybe for the summer, and frequently for holiday visits, but I knew for all intents and purposes, I was moving away. I suspect the same was true of those who left for a job and an apartment, for military service, and surely for those who left to marry.

Two factors contributed to this clear break. First, economics made it difficult for most families to continue support for a young person past the age of graduation, with the exception, of course, of agricultural or small business families. Young people who finished school were expected to carry their own weight. Those who remained at home were expected to contribute financially to household expenses. Second, young people themselves seemed anxious to move from the tight reins of home and into the challenge of independence.

Times have changed, however. The transition period in which the passage, the gateway, the bridge between adolescence and adulthood occurs seems enshrouded in a fog of uncertainty. More young people enjoy a higher level of affluence than ever before. Some of my middle-aged friends comment that their own parents grieved when they moved out; now as parents themselves, they grieve because their children won't move out. Why should these young people be in a hurry to move out? Many of them enjoy more luxury, much more independence, and a higher level of entertainment than they may ever enjoy on their own. Furthermore, the uncertainty of life due to nuclear threat, the environmental crises, and various diseases seem to have made young people insecure enough to hang around their cocoons.

The four-year period from high school graduation to college graduation, for those who indeed graduate in four years, does not always mean young adults are better equipped for responsibility; it may mean young adults are even more uncertain of their own future. The settling-down period in the 1980s has expanded into ten or twelve years, two or three enrollments in college and/or graduate schools, a half-dozen different jobs, and several returns to home in order to "get my head together." Young adults are waiting longer to marry, facing greater difficulties settling into careers, getting an education, leaving home, breaking financial dependencies and, in short, moving from adolescence into young adulthood.

The delay in settling into the normal patterns of adulthood experienced by increasing numbers of young people in their late twenties and early thirties indicates weaknesses in the kinds of direction society is providing. The hard truth may have something to do with the near total absence of assistance, or even the wrong kinds of direction and assistance.

In nearly every so-called primitive culture, the rituals connected with this transition begin about the time of sexual maturity and often lead directly into marriage and setting up a home. The purposes are clear and the methods well established. In Western culture at the end of the twentieth century, sophistication (or is it merely complications?) has made everyone uncertain about the exact time in which an adolescent actually becomes an adult. Young people see a driver's license and money from a part-time job as symbols of power which demonstrate the capacity for independence. Parents are reluctant to recognize that power as sufficient. These become years of tension between holding on and letting go. Sometimes the push and pull are overt, direct; at other times the need to control or be taken care of are so subtle that only careful examination is able to detect the mixed signals from parents and young adults.

Not infrequently, pastors and counselors face a young person whose relationship with his/her parents is suffering too much stress. Mom and dad won't let go; they give too much advice; they try to control everything. Young people may not even be aware that while resenting parental overinvolvement, they may be inviting that overinvolvement through some expectations of their own. The young woman may want her parents to recognize her as an adult, independent, able to support herself, but frequently drops hints about needing a washing machine or a new car. The garbled message is "Accept me as an adult/take care of me as a child." Unfortunately, that push/pull begins in mid teens and continues for many young adults well into their thirties.

Passage into young adulthood may take so long because of

an ill-defined set of standards or qualities society has for those called "adults." While no one segment of any culture decides such things, and while such things cannot be decided except over a long period of time, the church surely has a contribution to make in setting the standards for adulthood and in providing some of the rituals connected with the transition. The Bible, even though from another time and culture(s) provides much wisdom at this point.

Three Bible Characters

We can take some comfort in the fact that some of our most beloved Bible stories deal with the difficulty in the transition between youth and adulthood. I am always struck by the turmoil, violence, and pain which are part of this passage time—even in the biblical setting.

Joseph is timeless. Beginning with Genesis 37, he occupies a large portion of the biblical text. The pampered and favored son of his aged father, he was despised by his brothers. But for one squeamish brother, the others would have killed him. At first they placed him in a dry well to die. Then they pulled him out and sold him to some desert Bedoins for twenty shekels of silver. They told their father he had been killed by a wild animal. But Joseph went to Egypt with a multitude of skills and some depth of character. There, fully separated from his privileged life and completely dependent upon his own resources, he became a responsible adult of great power and character. Joseph was seventeen years of age when the transition occurred. His "rite of passage," if it could be called that, was anything but supported and encouraged; it was definitive. We can see the violence and the turmoil involved and have no difficulty finding parallels in modern times.

David appears in 1 Samuel 16 and never disappears from Hebrew Scriptures. Even after his death he continued to exert enormous influence upon his nation. David was another youngest son resented by his brothers and protected by his father. Joseph was the dreamer, par excellence, but David must have appeared to his brothers as an airhead in his own right. He took care of the sheep, played a harp, and wrote poems. When he appeared in the camp of Saul's men, he embarrassed his soldier brothers; when he volunteered to take on Goliath, his brothers may have been tempted to kill him. Yet, the real giant for this stripling may well have been that very battle to become an adult. He risked his life in a kind of initiation gauntlet. His rite of passage, like Joseph's, was violent beyond belief, but he was never again mistaken for a boy. He never again lived in the house of his father. Again, the tension and turmoil in the passage from adolescence to adulthood proved to be harsh. We all know contemporary examples of such struggles.

The prodigal son appears in Luke 15 in the context of three parables about God's mercy in the face of lostness. The lost son stands at least in part as a story of a boy who became a man in all the wrong ways, and finally did so only with the help of a wise and gracious father. No one faults the boy for wanting out from under the shadow of the elder brother and the constraints of even the best of fathers. He was a fool, not because he wanted his own life, but because he threw it away before he knew what it was. He cut himself off from home and tried to make a community where none was possible. Joseph and David took advantage of bad situations and struggled on their own to become men; the prodigal left under bad circumstances which he created, and almost destroyed himself. To his credit, he went back; to his shame, he went back to be less than he was when he left: he asked for job as a field hand!

Again, the violence, turmoil, and struggle to become an adult are all present in the story of the prodigal. But here, a wise father bided his time, held his grief, and finally offered direction on his own terms. When the boy was ready to learn, share responsibility, and relate as an adult, the party began. Could we say that the party was itself a ritual in the passage from adolescence to adulthood?

In all three characters, I am impressed by the difficulty of the passage to adulthood. I am taken by the demands of youth and the reluctance of parents. I am struck by the difficult balance between privilege and responsibility. Eventually, Joseph became father to his own father and brothers, David became father to his country, and the prodigal became a partner with his father. Yet, the bridge was narrow and long, always precarious for each of the three.

The Bible in such stories as these in its direct teachings, and in the Wisdom Literature, seems to recognize the painful process of becoming an adult. There may have been no high-school or college graduations, but there were schools of experience and recognitions of the high cost of the education. The accounts of the grief and the accomplishments are so archetypal, so primal, so universal, that we have no difficulty making the connections.

Because the Bible recognizes these transitions, the church will do well to take them seriously, also. Because of cultural differences and our own period of cultural change, the church is faced with a need to be involved in more creative ways than ever. Of all need times, the passage between adolescence and adulthood may be the most difficult, and the least attended to by the church. What, then, shall we do?

The Starting Point: Facing Reality

The first reality the church must face is the separation of sexual maturity from marriage. In many cultures, the rite of passage from youth to adulthood combines these two phenomena. The transition in such cases occurs relatively quickly. The line between childhood and adulthood have been clearly drawn. Everybody knows exactly where the one ends and the other begins. Not so in our culture. The period of time is extended; the line is wavy and often blurred. Even in our own culture a generation ago, the line was a bit clearer: graduation, a job and income, and usually marriage.

Now, substantial earning often precedes graduation, and education may include two or more graduations. The young adult may live at home, move out, or go back and forth. Our transient society often separates individuals from their extended families—those who "tell them who they are." Those who are independent in many ways remain in other areas quite dependent. Our society is no longer as clear about the time or event(s) in which an adolescent becomes an adult. One may "come of age" and yet still retain many of the characteristics of an adolescent. Our culture no longer expects young people to marry and assume the responsibilities of adulthood as soon as they become physically mature.

A second reality in this age of transition is what one researcher called "the postponed generation."[1] Even in this culture, where marriage has historically occurred much later than thirteen, fourteen, or fifteen, we are seeing everything pertaining to adulthood happening a decade or so later. Young adults are not fully adult in responsibility, independence, employment, marriage, and direction until much later than they were a generation ago. Susan Littwin gives four reasons for the delay:

1. Their expectations are too high. They want a very high salary, all the luxury money can buy, the perfect relationship, and total fulfillment.
2. The fast-paced world often means the job they prepare for is glutted by the time they get ready to work, or it is made

obsolete by technological changes. This generation is frightened by all these changes.

3. Male/female roles are equalizing and in some cases reversing. The models from the past generation may not be adequate in the present.

4. These young adults have been told over and over that they are special, but when they get "out there," they often find they must compete with hundreds of other "special people."[1]

These factors influencing the delay in the transition mean that the current generation of adolescents need help more than ever to interpret their future place in the adult world.

A third reality the church must face is the absence of these young people from the local churches. Most of them left at age sixteen when they got a job and a driver's license; often they don't come back until they marry, but then only for the wedding, and may not return until the birth of the first baby. Exceptions may be Easter and Christmas or when their parents come from another city or state to visit them. Frequently I am introduced at the door of the sanctuary following worship by the young couple who say, "Mom and Dad, I want you to meet our pastor." I find myself smiling and playing the part, unable to remember whether I saw the couple or young person on Christmas, Easter, or when they first moved to the community.

None of this is offered as criticism. It is simply the way things are. Some separation from the parent's faith is necessary if faith is to become their own. Just as marriage, a career, and full adult responsibility come later, so does personal commitment to faith and a local church. I suspect that just as young people between sixteen and the late twenties are not sure where they belong, neither does the church know how to make a place for them.

If the church learns to provide rituals of passage for

adolescents becoming adults, the church must first learn to deal with a bridge at least ten years long. Understanding will be needed instead of criticism, lamentation, and rejection. Young adults who have not fully embarked upon adulthood make up a new subculture. To their credit, many local churches try to establish singles groups, young married couples classes, and other young adult programs; they tend to find the success rate rather low and the frustration levels high. When we attempt to provide "rituals of passage" from adolescence to adulthood, we find that many rituals are needed over a long period of time. During this period in the life cycle more than any other, the church must become informed about what is happening to these population groups, exercise tremendous patience and persistence, and be creative.

Most churches tend to direct their resources to the youth programs—junior and senior high school age. While I believe those programs and that attention are vital, I wish the churches would direct equal energy toward young adults from the time they graduate from high school until they settle into full adulthood. These years are almost unrecognized for their need and the intensity of their struggle because these young adults have become so sophisticated in hiding their inner tensions. So, what kind of rites and rituals are available for this stage of development?

Rites of Passage

First, the bad news. I cannot envision any single formal ritual like baby dedication or baptism which marks clearly the passage from adolescence to adulthood. Birth and conversion take place in a very short span of time. In the free-church tradition, the line between lost and saved remains rather clear. In all faith traditions the line between prenatal and birth are even clearer! We can hardly be as sure about a moment, year, or event in which an adolescent becomes an adult. The time line is so long and the transition events so numerous that a series of rituals, formal and informal, will be needed.

Yet, these young adults, with all their ambivalence, reluctance, and uncertainty are vital to the culture and the church. Who knows but if this slow and painful transition is rightly supported these young adults may emerge better qualified to take their places of leadership in new and unheard ways. The church can have a significant hand in this long and often harsh transition.

So there is indeed good news. It begins before graduation. Wayne E. Oates observed many years ago that earning a driver's license is a pivotal event in the life of the teenager.[2] He expressed surprise that the church has not chosen to make more than we do over such an important event. Perhaps in the youth group of the local church, some ceremony should be devised to emphasize the weight of importance the young people themselves place upon this achievement. In the state of Virginia, every teenager must appear before a judge to receive a driver's license. I remember going with my daughter and sitting in the courtroom listening to a wise judge mix humor, preaching, and the law. My daughter was impressed with this secular ritual. I wished then that her youth director in the church could have witnessed the ceremony and devised one like it to recognize her and her peers as a part of their weekly meeting. That little card carried all sorts of implications for her, for her parents, and for society.

A second event is high-school graduation. In the secular world a great deal is made of both the achievement and the ceremonies. Many local churches have taken less interest in what is surely a milestone. By the eighteenth year much of the turmoil and tumult of early adolescence is past. Much of the task of identity, authority, and sexuality is clarified; while they remain largely uncompleted, the young people seem to have some direction about them. Some future purpose has begun to emerge toward additional schooling or some kind of employment. The caps and gowns, the awarding of diplomas, a sense of closure on a period in life, and some reaching out deserve ceremonial attention, and schools provide that. But what about the spiritual side of this transition?

Schools at one time attempted to provide this emphasis also. Baccalaureate ceremonies in the past offered prayers and a speech/sermon by a local minister. The changes in the sixties, spurred by protests by those who were offended by school-sponsored religion, led to the demise of such services in many school systems. Many of those schools which maintained such customs made attendance optional. Now, many high schools and some colleges are bringing such services back—at the request of the students. I interpret this renewed interest as recognition that graduation is far more than academic achievement. This event has spiritual as well as secular importance.

What can the local church do to recognize the importance of this passage from adolescence to early adulthood? One advantage of the free-church tradition is flexibility in worship, thus enabling some creativity in both themes and liturgy. My own Baptist tradition has such capability in devising programs to meet needs that we should uncover a multitude of ideas. I suggest a series of rituals/traditions which might emerge to facilitate this transition. These come from my own experience and my conversations with leaders in other churches.

The primary recognition may be a worship service designed with graduating seniors as the honorees. The pastor, the church musician, a leader from the youth group, and an adult sponsor of the youth group may meet to plan such a worship service. In larger churches, the youth choir may provide some of the music; if sufficient talent is available, youth vocalists and/or instrumentalists can lend their gifts in the service music. The pastor will have an exceptional opportunity to address the young people and to express appreciation to church leaders and to parents. The sermon may well emphasize the pilgrimage, the past, and present rewards.

During the response/invitation time, the graduating seniors may be called to the altar area for a presentation of a certificate of recognition and/or a token gift such as a New Testament inscribed to each young person and signed by an official of the church. Names of graduating seniors should appear in the printed worship bulletin. Included in this altar ceremony may be a litany of recognition or a prayer or both. The following is offered as a sample:

Minister: We, the family of God in this place, salute you in your accomplishments in personal growth and development, academics, and social skills. We recognize your struggles and your persistence in a period of your lives which has demanded effort and persistence.

Congregation: We are proud to have shared your journey, both as observers and as contributors. We remember with you the difficulties and the rewards. We thank you for the contributions you have made to us and continue to make to the world around you.

Minister: We offer thanks to God for the energy and optimism of your lives, and for the inspiration you are to all of us. Let us pray.

All: Lord God, who gives us courage of heart and strength of will to work with our hands and minds, receive our thanks for all learning and growing. Let us pause to rejoice in every plateau of our lives, and to share in the celebration. In great joy and sincere hope, enable us to serve Thee and Thy kingdom with all our hearts, minds, and spirits through Jesus Christ, our Lord. Amen.

Following the worship service a reception might be given for the seniors and their families, thus providing each member of the congregation an opportunity for a personal word of congratulations.

Another tradition established by some churches is the annual breakfast for seniors. I have heard of some very creative approaches, including slide shows or photographic collages put together with the help of friends and relatives. An event like this can be lighthearted and marked by humorous accounts of events in the lives of each senior during the high school years. If a breakfast is not convenient, some other meal or party can be given.

For many years I have written by hand a letter of congratulations to each graduate. I try to recall some event/ events in which I have related to each of them. While I close with a word of encouragement for the future, the theme of the letter is remembering the past and honoring the milestone and transition. I am not always aware of how the letters are received but I am given sufficient signals to let me know I am making some significant contact. In several cases, the letter has opened a door to future relationship which I had not been able to establish to that point. I think of one student who had been distant from me. After my letter, I began to hear frequently from this young person. She continues to write to me and always comes by my office to say hello when she visits her family.

These suggestions are by no means definitive. I offer them as examples of the kinds of rituals and traditions which may be effective. I am sure many ministers and lay leaders could add many more creative rituals, both formal and informal. The possibilities are unlimited. The important thing is that some effort be made to mark this significant transition in ways which underscore not simply graduation, but also the movement into or toward a new stage in the life cycle.

A third event in this adolescent-to-adulthood gateway has to do with going away, leaving home, setting up a greater degree of independence. The church I serve is located across the main street of town and directly opposite a major college. My study windows face the campus, including several residence halls. August is always a reflective time for me, but a bittersweet month for students and their parents. I watch vans and station wagons drive up to the curbs. The entire family comes along, often in another car. Everyone goes through the frustrations of carrying more things than those little rooms could possibly accommodate. I imagine the dads grumbling about the overabundance of stuff, the younger siblings complaining about having to carry somebody else's stuff, and the moms saying nothing because of the sadness they feel about a ritual of going away. Everyone feels the same things; each expresses those feelings differently.

The scenes are not limited to college campuses, however. Airports and train stations tell similar tales for those who leave for the military or for a job in a distant place. The mixtures of emotion include pride and sadness, excitement and anxiety. The intensity of these moments is surely drawn not simply from leaving home, going away, but also from the transition from adolescence to young adulthood. If graduation offers an opportunity for formal rituals, this going away also calls for some informal involvements by the local churches.

One means of involvement in this transition may be a system of ongoing contact between the young adult and the church. The most obvious communication remains the church newsletter. Mail makes every day a bit better, especially when we are far away from our roots. In the church I serve, many of the young people who move away let us know their addresses, even without the office asking for them; they are just as conscientious about notifying us of changes in address. They tell us they appreciate the newsletter. In a wry way, I think to myself that it is strange: we could never get our teenagers to read the newsletter, but when they leave home, they read it carefully. That little piece of mail provides a vital link with the past—as well as some sense of continuity in the present.

A second means of informal involvement which can become a significant ritual/tradition ought to be some regular and personal communication. Some years ago a church I served began to send "care" packages to those who graduated from high school and left the community. One was mailed in mid fall and another was sent in mid spring. They contained candy, toiletries, little toys and games, and gag gifts. Women's groups or youth groups will find that the young people will appreciate these gifts far beyond the level of their cost.

Another communication effort can last much longer. Each young person who graduates and goes away can be "adopted" by an adult in the church. I have seen this happen on a non-programmed basis and continue for years. Letters and cards are exchanged; when the young adult visits parents, he/she also visits the adult who has become a friend. I often see these young people, home for a visit, sitting in worship with an adult who became a friend in the transition period. With minimal effort, any church could expand these matches by promoting them, the quieter the better. Every effort should be made to avoid all appearances of a "program." Such matches are highly personal and delicate because they move into the adult-to-adult relationship level, sometimes for the first time where the young person is concerned.

Each church must be willing to risk failure in establishing these, or any rituals of transition and efforts at ongoing support. What may "work" for one church, may not be successful in another. Much depends upon lay leaders who will work with the professionals. The leadership needs to remain somewhat stable because the young people and their families are constantly new. For many years of ministry I was unable to relate existentially to parents whose young people were applying for jobs or colleges, graduating, leaving home, returning briefly. Now with two youngsters in this age group, I find myself understanding much more. I also realize, however, that in a period of about one decade, this particular transition will no longer hold center stage for me. So it is for others in the church. For this reason, the church will need to reassess both professional and lay involvement in these rituals so that some adults with deep emotional investment will always be available in these efforts. These leaders will provide a level of intensity and urgency needed to make the rituals all they need to be.

A Word About Other Family Members

The central characters in the faith rituals at the times of birth and death participate in very limited ways. In all the other rites of passage, the central characters are very aware and deeply invested. They are not, however, the only ones intimately involved. Nowhere is this more apparent than in the transition between adolescence and adulthood. The young person certainly carries some weight of anxiety about what lies ahead, but the parents nearly always struggle at much deeper levels.

We whose young people embark upon adulthood carry all sorts of emotional baggage. Have we given them enough of the right things? Are they leaving too early? Parents almost always think they are. How much should we be involved? It is the ever-present tension of let go-hold on. In establishing rituals of transition for the young people, some inclusions for involvement/recognition of other family members is needed. The simple expressions of sensitivity to parents who are struggling with perfectly normal self-doubts and grief may in itself be enough. They may be consulted, invited, mentioned in prayers and sermons, thanked. They should not be over-looked.

In every church, those who share a given life stage tend to be drawn together by their common experience; they are able to encourage one another, and they often do. The rituals may be formal or informal; they may be highly visible or intentional peripheral. They are all important to those leaving the most difficult period of their lives; they are vital for the generation of adults who receive them as new adults. Like every rite of passage, this one looks back and then ahead with a mix of emotions. Such explains the value of the rituals themselves.

Notes

1. Susan Littwin, *The Postponed Generation* (New York: Morrow, 1986).
2. Wayne E. Oates, *On Becoming Children of God* (Philadelphia: Westminster Press, 1969).

4
Marriage

"They shall be one flesh" (Gen. 2:24, KJV).

Of all the rituals connected with the passage from one life stage to the next, marriage is the most intentionally celebrative, the most exuberant, the most elaborate. At least in the "ideal," or model wedding, the kind described in the magazines, the kind we remember, weddings are extravaganzas. Banks of flowers and candles, beautifully colored and tailored dresses and tuxedos, the grandest music possible, all the sentiment which can be packed into the hour, and a magnificent party afterward!

Not every couple can afford such a celebration; not every couple who can afford it chooses it. Its relative importance depends upon who happens to be expressing an opinion. How often do we hear the bride or a member of her family say, "This is the most important day of my/her life and it should be as grand as possible!" I know of several fathers and mothers who have written checks for large amounts of money and have said, "You can use it all on the wedding or use a portion and keep the rest." In many cases, the couple chooses to use it all on the wedding. And "all" is often much. One father with a careful eye for numbers had kept the accounting of his daughter's wedding to the penny. At the conclusion of the twenty-one minute ceremony, he looked at his watch, paused for some calculations, leaned over to his wife and said, "$____.00 a minute!" Many weddings are indeed extravagant.

Because of the many details of the wedding, the number of people involved, and the myriad and powerful emotions which dance on the razor's edge during this time, the minister and the church and the couple often find this the most challenging of all the rites of passage. Not infrequently does the minister work in vain to penetrate the trappings of the wedding in effort to interpret the ceremony and prepare the couple for marriage. Yet, very often, the minister finds the couple deeply involved in such important issues themselves, and anxious for any help their pastor can give them.

In my own experience, the extravagance or simplicity of the wedding has little correlation with the couple's openness to interpretation by the clergy. I have officiated in some weddings of great extravagance in which I have had good feelings about the couple's seriousness and depth of perceptivity about the wedding and about marriage. I have participated in some very simple weddings in which I entertained all sorts of misgivings about the couple's understanding and intentions. Who can forget the high seriousness in the film version of *Roots,* when Kunta Kinte and his bride "jumped over the broom"! The wedding was the simplest of the simple; the seriousness was of the highest order.

The church can and should establish policies about who can be married under her canopy. The church can and should make every attempt to prepare the couple for both the ceremony and for marriage. The church must include the families of the couple in all her ministries. The church cannot, however, control the intentions or the level of seriousness with which they approach either the wedding or marriage. In weddings, as in every other function, the church ought to hold high the noblest ideals in the celebration of the marriage vows, and provide some direction for the growth of the couple in those promises. Some of the rituals which the church holds high can be prescribed and insisted upon; others can be offered as options. Some rituals will be in the hands of groups within the congregation and others will be the responsibility of the clergy. But the ideals should be emphasized by what are rules and standards of the church as well as rituals which have become traditions.

Such ideals can be held high if the rituals of preparation, the actual ceremony of marriage, and the welcoming process following the wedding are done with thoroughness and integrity.

Rituals of Preparation

The engagement announcement brings down upon the couple an incredible amount of work and many decisions about wedding details. The announcement becomes an invitation to the families and friends to pour forth an abundance of suggestions and requirements. Some may be categorized as opinions and preferences; others fall into the hopper of tradition—what our family has always done. Prospective brides tend to feel overwhelmed and their fiances tend to become frustrated along the way. The time of planning, however, enables the couple to find perspective, sort out the demands, and settle on a process. The faith community provides a canopy of tradition and protection under which a couple can find both calm and direction. The officiating minister stands at the center of the umbrella of both faith and order.

The pastor serves everyone well when establishing clearly the requirements of the church in all weddings. The saddest characteristic of the "free-church tradition," unfortunately, is that everyone tends to do as they please. In weddings that often means disaster. Those who say everyone has a right to be married and buried as they please are correct only within limits. They must observe the civil laws. The church, too, should have clearly defined expectations. If these are carefully established, and consistently and gracefully followed, most families will be aware of them well in advance of their own wedding, and appreciate the structure they provide.

I endorse wholeheartedly the requirement of many pastors that the couple participate in a series of preparatory sessions. I require three one-hour meetings but these often expand to four or five at the request of the couple. On occasions, in which one or both in the couple lives or works out of town, I will arrange two hour-and-a-half sessions. These are usually prefaced by a call from the woman to tell me about the engagement, to ask if the sanctuary is available on the date they have chosen, and if I can/will officiate. I prefer to set up an appointment with her (or both of them) as soon as possible, for several purposes.

In that preparation-for-preparation meeting, I want to celebrate with them their engagement and informally bless their excitement and happiness of the moment. I also want to establish what I understand as my role in their wedding. The church, the organist, and I each have available copies of individual wedding policies, stating clearly what is offered, and in a few matters what is unacceptable. Those who believe that everyone should be allowed to be married and buried as they choose would surely find "wedding policies" offensive. Yet, the integrity of the church, of marriage, of worship, of the clergy, and of church musicians are all involved. Such policies ought to have grown out of respect for Christian marriage, as well as from experience in what is good, right, and appropriate. Such policies are desperately needed, enormously helpful.

Every minister has a sack full of stories about wedding oddities. Some are hilarious foibles of human imperfection.

Many are sad testimonies to bad theology and spiritual insensitivity. I have been asked to perform a ceremony of marriage in which the name of God was to be omitted and no prayers offered. I have been asked to read poems which were not only poorly written but heretical in theology or questionable in morality. I have also been embarrassed for the church by some of the music I have heard performed as a part of a wedding/worship service.

If the pastor can become an early contributor to wedding planning, the couple can be spared choices they may regret in years to come. Therefore, if I can set up a meeting with the couple to be married, and do so very early in the planning process, I can bring the best traditions of the church to bear upon a particular ceremony. So after my time of congratulations and celebration of the engagement, and a discussion of wedding policies, I provide information about the ceremony itself.

I give them a copy of the ceremony I use and point out that I am flexible and willing to make many changes in order to personalize it. I also point out that since the ceremony is a worship service, some changes and/or inclusions may not be appropriate to a Christian wedding and these would need to be negotiated carefully. Such an approach establishes ground rules and opens the door to discuss later every detail and word in the ceremony. I offer to provide some poems, a list of Scriptures and some worship format alternatives if they would like this kind of direction. More specific discussions of all these issues are then put aside until the first scheduled meeting.

The final purpose of this "announcement" session is to explain the agenda for the three preparation sessions. I explain that they will be asked to fill out a personality profile which I will score and interpret for them, and that we will discuss their personality similarities and differences and what these may contribute to their marriage. I assure them that I try to do this in a positive way, but some characteristics are such that the interpretation becomes a kind of caution about potential problems. I explain that the sessions will deal with communication, decision making, problem solving, and conflict management, relationships with their respective families, and commitment. The approach and content will differ with each minister, but such a preliminary meeting should be held.

This meeting should be positive, upbeat, and optimistic. More than anything, the minister should try to convey a sense of partnership with the couple in an exciting journey of preparation for the wedding and for a life together. If the minister can convey a spirit of caring, a high degree of confidence in the value of the expectations, and a willingness to be available to the couple, the preparation sessions will prove to be themselves a celebration of sorts. Many couples complete these, admit they began with some anxiety, and express deep appreciation for my expenditure of time and personal sharing.

If such sessions seem demanding of a pastor's already overloaded schedule, I can offer some suggestions for limited relief. Occasionally, when I have several couples scheduled to be married in the summer, I offer the first two preparation sessions as group meetings. I include all the didactic material in these, especially a general interpretation of the personality profile. This means that I am able to save several hours of meetings and allow the couples being married in the same time frame to meet one another, exchange ideas, and share some of the others' celebration.

How does the church feel about the pastor taking a position of mandatory preparation sessions? Again, my own experience has been positive. Parents of the couples have been uniform in their appreciation of this kind of help. The couples themselves, however, nearly always enter the process with some skepticism—additional tasks connected with getting married, fear of the sessions invading their privacy, a distaste of preaching/advice, and uneasiness in the face of the unfamiliar. But the wise pastor knows that one always earns the right to be heard. Marriage is not easy as everyone knows. So the pastor should approach these sessions carefully, earning the acceptance of the couple. Sensitive pastors will find most couples, their families, and the church itself encourage any effort in sound preparation. Nevertheless, each minister will have much to say about how these requirements are received by the church.

The minister should not, however, be the sole representative of the church in the preparation rituals. The congregation has a part in the preparation process also. In many communities, bridal showers contribute to the preparation process; they are almost rituals in themselves. Singles groups and Sunday School classes in the church can and do provide powerful affirmations of the couple with parties and gifts. What is a most welcome change seems to be an increase of such showers, luncheons, and dinners given for the couple rather than for the woman by herself. These parties enlarge the number of people involved in preparation. These social rituals often bring together the faith community and those the couple have known apart from the church; the circle of support is enlarged and strengthened.

In smaller communities where the extended family has remained in tact, the cost of weddings is kept managable through spreading around the responsibilities. Someone bakes the wedding cake; another does the flowers; still another makes the dress(es). One group hosts a rehearsal dinner and another group does the reception. Not only is the expenditure of money lessened, the sense of participation is expanded and the expression of support and encouragement are sometimes overwhelming. A true sense of community is maintained.

In our changing culture where people are often mobile and separated from their roots, such participation and support have diminished. The church must work harder to broaden the network of involvement in the preparation process. Smaller church groups may find opportunities to assume the role of extended family through contributions such as showers or through volunteer assistance in the wedding details.

Part of the preparation rituals should include some discussion of the place of the church membership in the wedding. In that same transient nature of contemporary society, the church has sometimes taken on the role of the wedding chapel. The church members may not even be aware of a wedding on a given Saturday, or know the couple. Many couples are married in the church sanctuary but not in the context of the church family. As a ritual of passage under the canopy of faith, the wedding needs to include intentionally the body of Christ. What is the couple leaving in their passage? To what is the couple going? Who and what serves as bridge from one condition or state of being to the other?

In recent years I have found myself standing in the sanctuary I know so well, looking at a congregation of strangers. A few of them I met the night before at the rehearsal and the dinner; most I will meet for the first time at the reception. Where is the congregation I worship with each Sunday? These marriages I solemnize in this sanctuary I know so well must often be done apart from the body of Christ usually gathered here. If the couple comes to the altar from among the church usually gathered in this place, should not the church be present, involved? Should not these guests who are strangers to us be welcomed and made at home by those whose home church this is? If the church is not present, who

welcomes the guests? If the church is not present, how can
the couple come to the altar from among them?

Over a period of six months I discussed these questions
with many of the leaders of the church I now served. I believe
we agreed that weddings in our church demand of us all
some significant level of support beyond the official role of
the pastor and organist, and the use of the sanctuary. We
discussed the value and problems of the custom of the open
church. In the end, the church voted to ask each couple
married in our sanctuary to publish in the church newsletter
an invitation to the wedding. Many people in the church
agreed that the church needs to be represented by more of
the church family. In weddings solemnized since that practice began, I have noticed an increase of attendance by
church leaders. I hope the couples felt a significant level of
support.

Of course, the problem of the planning and cost of the
reception, especially if held in the church fellowship hall,
becomes more difficult. Furthermore, when a general invitation is published and invitations are mailed as well, some
within the church will receive personal invitations and others
will not. Each local church will do well to discuss the involvement of the congregation and work out these problems.
The important issue, however, is that of congregational presence and support in the transition. Such discussions can only
lead to a deeper understanding of the rule of the church in
times of life-cycle transition.

The Wedding Ceremony as Primary Marriage Ritual

"We are here assembled to worship God and join (name)
and (name) in holy matrimony." Holy matrimony! Such is
our heritage. That so many—Christians and non-Christians
alike—come to the altar of God to be married is explained
by much more than the power of custom. *Holy* matrimony

says something about the place of God in sealing the vows. The very image of marriage has for centuries served to join divine and human hands. Israel was seen as bride of God (Ps. 45; Isa. 54:6; Hos. 2:19-20; Ezek. 16:8, etc.). The church has often been called the Bride of Christ. (Rev. 21:2,9). New believers are "born again" into that relationship, becoming "brothers and sisters" within the household of God. Jesus Himself used the marriage/wedding images in His teaching (Matt. 9:15; Mark 2:19; etc.). He began His ministry by attending the marriage at Cana (John 2). Marriage and weddings provide a powerful image for the divine/human relationship.

The church and her ministers are called upon to solemnize weddings because marriage is thought of in terms of a divinely ordained institution. As such, the expectations and fears connected with marriage seem to cry out for the blessing of God. Samuel Johnson commented offhandedly that marriage is the most unnatural institution, demanding all the laws of God and mankind to keep it together. Every couple knows the difficulties that lie ahead; they have watched problems and failures trouble the marriages of others—perhaps even those of their own parents. But somehow "in my marriage," they say, "things will be right," especially if we bring God into it.

Marriage vows stand on a higher plane than mere promises. Marriage is holy and wedding rituals must underscore that sanctity. The church is the setting. The minister represents the faith community and serves a priestly function as well. All the symbols of faith are directed to this transitional time of leaving the unmarried state, the homes of fathers and mothers, and crossing the bridge to a new relationship within their own home and family. As God presided over the union of the first man and woman, so in the church we ask God to preside over the unions of all the sons and daughters of the first couple. Marriage is holy and the ceremony which solemnizes the marriage is a service of worship.

D. Elton Trueblood saw in the late 1940s some tendencies which today make him appear to have been a modern-day prophet. He talked about marriage being an unconditional relationship: commitment rather than contract.[1] So the vows unapologetically include "richer and poorer," "for better for worse," "in sickness and health," "forsaking all others," for "as long as we both shall live." No longer possible? Some would agree in light of a changing world and the gradual shifting of the roles of both men and women within this changing world. Yet God's commitment to us models our attempts at unconditional relationship in marriage.

Because marriage requires a higher level of commitment than mere promise, the ceremony for the people of God must ever be sacred rather than secular. If before God the vows are exchanged and in prayer they are sealed, the place is an altar, be it sanctuary, garden, or living room. When the couple asks for the privilege of clergy, they must assume a sacred ceremony and the clergy must assume all the resources of faith will be brought to bear upon the ritual.

Trueblood went on to insist that marriage is public and not private.[2] The community has a stake in the union, in monogamy, in the children to come from that union. Marriage suggests relationships beyond the couple because the couple shares in the interconnected responsibility of the social order. The commitments emphasized in the marriage ceremony may be first of one partner in the marriage to the other; it is also commitment of the couple to the community and the community to the couple; and that commitment extends to children who may be born into that new family.

We might add that the ceremony of marriage emphasizes certain bonds, fetters, at the expense of other freedoms. While the couple retains individuality and uniqueness, each surrenders a portion of the freedom experienced outside of marriage. When such fetters are resisted, broken, or violated, the sacred relationship, as well as the social order, is damaged.

What sorts of ceremonies and embellishments to those ceremonies are appropriate to such a vital passage? I must confess to a model by which I have measured all marriage ceremonies. The model, until a few years ago, existed only in my mind. I envisioned a couple for whom faith and the church were central being married as a part of the Sunday morning worship service. Not every couple could naturally and appropriately fit their ceremony to this setting. However, when a particular middle-aged couple came to me to announce their wedding and to ask me to officiate in the ceremony, the model came to life. After some extensive negotiation, we managed to fit the ceremony I customarily use to the liturgy of our Sunday morning worship service.

Our worship often includes a processional of choir and ministers. The wedding party took its place in the regular processional. Early in the service the couple stood from their place on the front pew and responded to the statements of intent. The Scripture lessons and sermon addressed the subject of marriage. Vows were exchanged at the customary time of commitment in the regular worship service. The wedding party and choir recessed at the usual time.

Many people in the church contributed to an enormously successful service. The choral and organ music was carefully chosen and prepared, almost as a gift to the couple. The church members prepared a bountiful reception, which followed the service. My colleague who had been their pastor before he retired, shared in the official duties. Because of the place this couple enjoys in the community, the church overflowed, people stood along the walls, and some had to be turned away at the door. For months that followed people in the community stopped me to talk about the significance of such a wedding.

This is not to suggest that all weddings should take place in this way. Most could not, for a variety of reasons. I relate this experience to underscore the model: joyous celebration and solemn worship, as well as broad-based congregational involvement. This couple traveled together the pathway from being single to being married; they left something and they entered something else. They did so, I believe, with the blessing of God and in the company of their brothers and sisters in faith. As I envision every ceremony of marriage, this is what I wish could happen, even though the structure, time, and circumstances may not be the same.

Some subtle adjustment to most of the weddings I attend could result in movement toward the model I have suggested. The first of these concerns *the music*. Because the minister is the "official" (officiant) in the wedding, and an authority in the area of worship, the minister needs to exercise more direction in the music of the ceremony. If the minister is not knowledgeable in music, the church musician should take that leading role. The minister and the church musician ideally need to work together at this point. The music chosen ought to benefit worship. In my preparation conferences, I remind the couple of this fact. I often challenge them to look ahead ten or twenty years and think about whether or not a particular piece of music is likely to be as meaningful to them then. I ask to what extent the pieces they choose will magnify the God we worship. I ask them to consider whether or not the music is merely sentimental or if it appeals to the total person. Most couples need and appreciate some specific direction in the planning of something they have never done before, especially in matters of music about which they may know very little.

Not only am I concerned to avoid bad music and encourage appropriate music, I suggest that the couple consider congregational singing. In most weddings the congregation is an audience—spectators. Hymn singing involves them in a beautiful way. A hymn may be chosen as processional or recessional music, or as music by which the couple lights the unity candle.

A second subtle adjustment to the usual ceremony picks up the issue of *congregational participation.* In addition to hymn singing, the Lord's Prayer ought to be included (if not used as a musical solo) as a part of the prayer of dedication (following the vows).

Another possibility for congregational involvement is a litany. Following the couples' statements of intent ("Will you take this woman/man. . . ."), a covenant question should be addressed to the father and mother of the bride, and the father and mother of the groom. A similar question of covenant can be addressed to the congregation. This covenant section can be a kind of responsive litany. If a bulletin is printed, a responsive prayer can be included to involve the congregation. Most hymnals include responsive readings of Scriptures; these should also be considered.

Since the wedding is a passage from some state or condition to another, and since the congregation is made up of those who are a part of the transition, they need to be heard from, both actually and symbolically.

A third subtle adjustment/addition concerns a variety of *symbols* which punctuate various parts of the worship. The first of these is the unity candles. Following the vows and before the prayer of commitment, the couple may approach a triple candelabra which symbolizes the oneness that comes from the two. In many cases, the couple chooses to have their parents light the two candles just before the procession. The minister must take care to talk about this symbol in the preparation time. I recall a wedding in which the couple lit the center candle and blew out their individual candles. I was aghast. They do not lose their individuality and uniqueness when they marry—or at least, they should not!

Another symbolic act comes after the pronouncement of husband and wife and either before or after the benediction. The couple may present a flower to each set of parents. If the bride gives the flower to her parents, she may be symbolizing leaving them gracefully; the same for the groom and his parents. If they choose each to present the flower to the other's parents, the symbol may be one of inclusion.

A third symbol is that of the rings. I tend to be reluctant to explain any symbol. After all, we choose symbols to say more eloquently than words what we need to convey. To explain a symbol may risk diminishing its power or insulting the congregation. Nevertheless, as a personal message to the couple, I comment on the rings. The gold suggests the growth of love from the rough ore to its refined stage, and the heat of difficulty which is required in the process. The luster of the gold suggests the friction by which the true quality becomes visible and brilliant. "Leiben and arbieten," said Freud: "Love and work." The rings on loving and working hands remain lustrous. Finally, the shaping of the near liquid gold into seamless rings suggests love which has no beginning and no ending. This ring message serves as a challenge to the couple to see their relationship in terms of the Love made flesh, the incarnation of perfect love.

Obviously, symbols must be judiciously chosen and carefully used. When done well, the inspiration continues as a part of the consciousness of everyone involved.

The physical setting—the sanctuary—also contributes to the ritual of marriage. Most sanctuaries, continuously set for worship, require less adornment for weddings than many people think. When so much greenery, candles, and flowers are used that the identity of the religious sanctuary is lost, what was intended as beauty becomes gaudiness. Simple in most cases is better, less expensive, and unpretentious.

A final word, then, about the ceremony as a bridge between what is left behind and what is ahead. The exchange of vows is the apex of the wedding. Wherever possible, and this often depends upon the architecture of the sanctuary, the couple ought to separate themselves from the wedding party.[3] The processional is an act of separation from the congregation; the blessing by the parents is an act of separation from the family of origin; the vows before the minister should be the final movement—from the wedding party—toward God. If at all possible, the couple should memorize their vows and repeat them without interruption. The couple, following the prayer of commitment and the lighting of the unity candle, will then return, first to the wedding party, and then to the congregation/community, as a couple rather than alone or as a member of their parents' household.

Rituals of Inclusion

The preparation rituals and the ceremony of transition give way to rituals by which the couple take their place in the community as a new family unit. They are sometimes reluctant to leave the households of their families of origin. The families are often reluctant to let go of them. The community sometimes accepts them quite slowly as adults comprising a new family. The faith community can make some contributions to this process.

The most formal ritual I know takes place on the first Sunday the couple returns to church following the wedding. In the welcoming time of the service the minister can welcome the couple for the first time in worship as husband and wife, Mr. and Mrs. (name). If such a custom is established in the church, the couple will know to expect such an introduction. Until the custom is established, the minister should arrange the introduction beforehand so as not to unduly embarrass them.

A second ritual of recognition, inclusion, and reception ought to be a visit to the new home by some official person in the church. The ideal person would be the minister but seldom can this leader make many calls of this nature. Another staff member, or two of the more prominent lay leaders can serve in this function. Whoever visits should state carefully the nature of the mission. "We have come in behalf of the church to offer congratulations in your marriage and to welcome you as a new family in the church." Information about a couple's Sunday School class can indicate further the new direction this couple will take within the faith community they already know.

In the church I serve, many of the couples arrange to leave altar flowers for the Sunday worship service. We include in the worship bulletin an acknowledgement of the flowers and the wedding. In the church newsletter the following week, we print a congratulatory note about the marriage.

Such rituals are simple and require very little effort. They are vital, however, because they say symbolically that the church does not wish to preside over a wedding which turns out to be a departure from the church family. The months and perhaps years following the wedding are full of difficulties for the couple. They will together renegotiate and struggle to earn a place in their community as competent adults, as a married couple/family unit. Much of this effort will, of necessity, be their own, but the church can provide them certain recognition and encouragement. If the church has been involved in the rituals of birth, baptism, and graduation, it will have already earned credibility sufficient to assist with the incorporation of this new family. The more intentional the rituals, the more effective the inclusion.

Notes

1. D. Elton Trueblood, *The Common Ventures of Life* (New York: Harper and Row, Publishers, 1949) pp. 42-44.

2. Ibid, pp. 46*ff.*

3. M. Mahan Siler, "Rites of Passage: A Meeting of Worship and Pastoral Care," *Review and Expositor,* Winter, 1988, p. 58.

5
Retirement

"Othello's occupation's gone" (*Othello*, William Shakespeare).

Al was a brother of a member in the church I served. I had heard Al and his wife mentioned several times. They had bought a house and a few acres of land in the community and planned to come south to retire. During a visit to the home of my church-member friend, I met Al and his wife; they were visiting for a week, trying to get the house redecorated for the move. The next time I heard from Al was a phone call several months later—from a large hospital in a nearby city: his tearful wife was asking me if I could come to the hospital right away.

Retirement had come one day and the moving van the next. But what had appeared to be an exciting new chapter in their lives proved disastrous. Al was diagnosed as having untreatable cancer; after a few months of excruciating pain, Al died. His wife was left to complete the process of emptying boxes—in still another house—all alone.

Isolated case? Probably not. Every minister has such stories. Not all are as terrible. Sometimes they relate how a person retires, begins to retreat from life, suffers emotional and physical deterioration, and dies earlier than we think he/she should have. Sometimes they require but can't find enough of the right things to keep them significantly busy. Sometimes they retire and tensions begin to erupt with their spouses or other family members. Sometimes they retire but cannot stay away from the job or the place they left.

Some cannot retire at all. Some of our favorite athletes continue to play their sport long after their skills have left them, and their fans remember their declining years more than their heroic ones. Ministers and other professional people also fall victim to the need to hold on too long. I feel some sadness in the memory of a minister whose sermons meant much to me—when he was at his best—but whose preaching deteriorated as surely as Al's diseased body. Many around us never quite come to grips with retirement. For those who do not, retirement turns destructive.

A Recent Phenomenon

The reason so many people have such difficulty with retirement seems to have less to do with too little money than with too much unfilled or insignificantly filled time. We should not be surprised since retirement is a relatively recent phenomenon and our society has not yet learned fully what to do with it.

In the not-too-distant past, few could afford to leave their work. Most who left were forced out by poor health, and many of these suffered economic hardship in their final years. For years after Social Security came into being, in 1935, the amount of money available remained too little to live on. Companies with retirement plans were few and many of those provided only meager incomes. Now, increasing numbers of people retire at earlier ages with more and more income. The employers' retirement programs, coupled with Social Security and individual savings, have made possible a comfortable life-style for increasing numbers of senior adults. Some are financially able to retire as early as their mid fifties.

Now, more than at any time in our history, the retirement ceremony, the gold watch, and the jokes about perpetual fishing or golf or travel close out a personal era of work. For some retirees, the picture is good. The hobbies and the travel trailer and the grandchildren and gardening and volunteer work make the senior years as fulfilling and even as productive as the years of "gainful employment."

But not always. I've often wondered if Al's cancer was triggered by a retirement he did not really want. I've occasionally known couples who found in retirement that they had grown far apart and no longer knew each other. I know several who feel they are no longer needed, who are angry at being replaced at a larger salary by a young person with far less experience, knowledge, and expertise. I meet senior adults who resent busywork often attached to retirement.

What may be more painful, especially for men, may be the subtle implication that if we have no work, we have no identity. In our culture, our work tends to identify us. The first thing we are asked by a new acquaintance is what we do or where we work. When we are introduced, we are summarized with, "She is a housewife," or homemaker, teacher, clerk, or whatever. If our identity resides in our work and our work is terminated, even by a retirement we have earned, we become nobody. Intellectually we can tell ourselves this is nonsense; emotionally, we tend to feel unattached, no longer needed, unidentified. Several retired career military officers live in my community. I notice many of them have their names and last rank posted on the mailboxes, and the little abbreviation for retired: "ret." At least, they take some identification with them into retirement. Doctors and ministers retain their titles, but most workers do not. For many people the loss of employment is not all fun and games, and may not even be a time of honor and respect.

The church has a role to play in providing a theology of vocation, in putting one's work into some larger perspective, in helping with the transition between leaving and arriving, and in reinterpreting the importance of each person in this new level of activity. The church may also have something to say about how the wisdom, experience, energy, and compassion characteristic of those in these "golden years" can be celebrated and directed. But the church is faced with learning about the dynamics of senior adulthood, especially its particular problems and needs. If such attention is given to this segment of our population, the rituals connected with leaving one's career and arriving at a new calling can be rewarding for the church and for those who retire.

Toward a Theology of Personhood, Work, and Vocation

Healthy and fulfilling retirement ought to be connected with a good theology of personhood, work, and play. For most of us, such an understanding comes about gradually. Perhaps the best lesson is found in the creation story and the Garden of Eden. The first couple received their value, their worth, not by the jobs they were given, but by virtue of their identities as those made in the image of God. As persons made in God's image, their importance seemed assured. As long as they lived in proximity to God, their work became a natural expression of who they were. When they fell from that relationship, their work became a mere means of their sustenance. Human beings have struggled since with the issues of identity and role; sadly, role has often provided identity.

Furthermore, what we know about God includes something about God's own work. As loving and caring Creator,

God shows Himself as One who gives. That work of creation stands as one expression of benevolence toward the created order. Yet God's identity stands alone, does not depend upon His "work" to say who He is. An even greater gift is God's willingness to take human beings into partnership; we are invited to share in the ongoing work of creation. And, finally, every work, profession, and vocation we undertake which contributes to the common good and shares in the partnership of God is sacramental—that is, sacred and honorable.

Several years ago Studs Terkel wrote a book entitled, *Working.*[1] He interviewed hundred Americans about their jobs. Terkel discovered that most people like their jobs, take pride in what they do, and believe they contribute to the well-being of their society. If Terkel had used theological language, he might have said these people have a sacramental view of their work. In 1949 D. Elton Trueblood wrote about what he called, *The Common Ventures of Life,*[2] birth, marriage, work, and death. He took the position that ministers are not the only people called by God to do God's work. Trueblood said in the chapter on "Work," and later in a 1952 book, *Your Other Vocation,*[3] that God calls all manner of people to all kinds of work; whatever we do to honor God and share in the ongoing creation of God is not just a job, it is a vocation, a calling.

When Jesus called some of his disciples to become "fishers of men" (Matt. 4:18-22), he was not calling them from bad or unacceptable work to a good work; he called them to change vocations. Paul was trained as a tentmaker. Even when he became a full-time missionary, he practiced his trade as a means of supporting himself and others who worked with him. Honorable work in partnership with God is a vocation, a calling. Many kinds of work can be vocations. Many people choose their work as a result of what they understand to have been God's call.

Such a sacramental view of work is central to retirement, especially to those who see retirement as a change in vocation. Such a view of work enables the worker to derive a sense of worth from God and sense of fulfillment from the calling. Any rituals of passage from one vocation to another, in partnership with God, enables celebration of what has been and anticipation of what is yet to be.

Closely aligned with the theology of personhood and the theology of work is a theology of play. Perhaps the best term is "recreation" or "re-creation." The more we know about pressure and stress, the more importance we place upon time and activity away from whatever causes stress. Indeed, for many people, a love of their work is more stress reducing than stress inducing. But even work deeply loved can create physical exhaustion and emotional saturation. Time away can be objective distance, important for evaluation. Distance can also provide some sense of balance to life in that we can see a composite picture. Our lives include work and worship, people and products, achievement and evaluation. Even God rested on the seventh day; His pause serves as our example.

Those who retire from their life's work and do so most successfully are those who have known how to make spaces in their work. They are people who during their working years enjoyed a variety of interests and activities. To expect someone who has known only work to be able at sixty-five to learn only play promises frustration and/or failure. The woman who could never find time to sew or play golf during her employment years will probably have difficulty taking up such activities in retirement.

Many years ago I was asked to write an article about preparing for retirement. I was surprised by the invitation so I wrote the editor of the periodical and asked why he would choose a young man who knew little about aging and thought little about retirement to do this article. He explained that he wanted a young person's impressions. I accepted the assignment and went to several persons whom I knew were happily retired. I asked them to tell me why they enjoyed retirement. Every one of them, using different stories and examples, told me the same things. They had always worked hard but maintained a variety of extra work interests. They all enjoyed work but looked forward to vacations and their other activities. When retirement time came, they had their hobbies, interests, and activities already in place and functioning. They had learned to do other things during their years of employment; when they had more time, they simply focused that resource more intensely upon the play they seemed never to have been able to do enough of. During their careers, their play renewed their work. When retirement came, they seemed already prepared, already involved in many rewarding activities. Retirement from work never seemed to mean retirement from life; it proved to be a matter of leaving one aspect of life and devoting more of themselves to issues, activities, and relationships already important to them. Preparation for retirement had been going on for years.

The Church and Retirement

Some move into retirement unprepared and filled with a sense of sadness, loss, and even fear. Others retire with remarkable enthusiasm to a long period of productivity and contribution. The church sees retirees at both ends of the spectrum and all through the middle. However, because this phenomenon of retirement, especially in the prime of life, is so new to our culture, the church has not yet fully come to grips with her role in the passage from gainful employment to a period in which one has a free hand in managing all twenty-four hours of every day.

Neither has the church done enough to interpret work in

light of retirement or to assist in the management of all the resources of life in retirement. The best we have done may be the provision of some activities for senior adults. I applaud senior adult groups which arrange recreational bus trips to vacation spots. Much can be said for the formation of a senior adult choir or a rhythm band using kitchen utensils. Nevertheless, such activities may prove to be little more than "something to do" in the absence of in-depth explorations and activities which emphasize the value of life at a very important age.

The church should pay much more attention to the time of passage, to that bridge from one state of being or activity to another. The church could serve well in the important function as celebrant to some of the actual ceremonies of retirement, as well as be participant in the nonchurch-sponsored ceremonies. Our society has long criticized business and industry for getting rid of used-up employees by simply sponsoring a retirement dinner and presenting the retiree with a gold watch and a few inane jokes. In truth, the church does even less to help our people prepare for retirement and then to help them make the transition. If we believe one's work is a vocation, a calling, an aspect of ministry in the marketplace, should not any transition in vocation be somehow marked and honored by the church?

The difficulty goes beyond simply learning about issues associated with retirement and aging, living longer and healthier, retiring earlier. The difficulty has further to do with the limitations of the church's pastoral ministry resources within worship and apart from worship. The planning calendar of the church can hardly stand another Sunday devoted to a special feature. Sundays prior to and around Christmas are filled with traditional emphases. Six Sundays before Easter and several Sundays after Easter are practically set in concrete. The period between Mother's Day and Father's Day include family emphases, memorial services, and graduations. Fall includes all kinds of program kickoffs and stewardship themes. Add to all that a heavy denominational schedule and the local church is standing at fifty-three Sundays and still counting. Any suggestion that the church add another ritual emphasis to the worship calendar appears to be more bad news than good.

The same difficulties appear when we look at suggested programs of preparation to help people get ready for retirement or interpret retirement. Most churches are already overprogrammed. Most church staff members are already over-burdened with program responsibilities. Any attempt to deal with the issue through a program in one of the regularly scheduled groups often turns out to be superficial.

If worship and program calendars are stressed, so are the pastoral-care resources. As much as every pastor would like to address every need of every parishioner, too many needs remain unattended. Pastors must choose the most critical problems and address those, wishing for more time, energy, or help. Little is ever done in the way of "preventive maintenance." So, what does the church do with an identified need and a vital message when time and energy run short?

I wish I had a ready solution to those problems because our congregation and staff also face them constantly. We all need to admit honestly our limitations, but at the same time continually reevaluate what we do in both worship and programming. In many cases, choices are made more difficult because we seldom choose between good things and bad; we must choose between the good and the best. Therefore, and in spite of the pressures upon the churches and their resources, some occasions and means should be found to help with the needs of this segment of our population. As the percentage of retired persons increases in our society, the opportunities and urgencies will compound. So where do we begin?

I would like to suggest the Sunday closest to Labor Day as a possible time to focus attention upon work and retirement. The theme for such a service would be "Christian Vocation." Resources for preaching on this topic are plentiful. Since work is vital to everyone, every member of the congregation will be involved in the theme. Perhaps ironically, such an emphasis will address most existentially those at each end of the age spectrum. Young people involved in vocational decisions will probably be alert to any discussion of the spiritual foundations for employment, careers, and work. Adults near retirement age and those who have retired should be anxious for help to interpret the next stage of their lives. God's call to work and God's involvement in one's work raises the theme to a high level.

The needs of young people just now looking to their careers have something to say about how the church deals with retirement and theology of work. My own ministry includes work with college students, so I know something about the anxieties and excitement of this age when they think about their careers. I look out my study window to a large campus. Students come for consultation. I speak to them in various settings. I see them in all sorts of campus and community activities. I meet their families. I try to listen to them. Because I am sometimes troubled by what I see and hear, I frequently ask professional colleagues in other such communities how they assess the student mind-set. My own concerns are neither narrow nor isolated. A seminary professor summed it up. I asked him how he assesses students in the 1980s compared with those of twenty-five years earlier. He mused aloud about what seemed to be a limited commitment to study, research, and ideas. He mentioned seminary as a credentialing institution: many attend not to learn but in order to qualify for a job. He mentioned a preoccupation with career paths, prestige, pay, and benefits. And then he said, "There seems to be little sense of vocation."

Young people beginning careers in the 1980s often seem to lack a sense of the call of God. The same may also apply across the board in the university, small college, seminary, and professional schools such as law, business, and medicine. If these generalizations, undocumented by hard research, are true, it does little good to search for a scapegoat. A better approach as far as the church is concerned is to address a problem and answer a need. Could it be that the church simply has not done a good job since the 1950s of addressing the issue of work through the "doctrine" of Christian vocation? I certainly feel a personal sense of that failure.

What better place, then, to begin to address the issue than around a "secular" holiday designated to honor work and workers? A sermon about vocation can be directed to everyone, both as a celebration of work and as an opportunity to instruct about the specifically Christian theology of work. Related issues may include the rights and responsibilities of both worker and employer, justice and equity in the work and marketplaces, and the Christian's witness in the secular setting.

Such a worship setting provides opportunity for preaching about retirement, although a "retirement" sermon would not be needed every year. What may become a tradition is a time in this service to recognize those in the membership of the church who have retired since the last such service. Much or little may be done with such a ceremony. At the least, the name and occupation of each person could be listed in the worship bulletin or on an inserted sheet. The number of years at the last job held and the person's title may also be included. Their names can be called and they may be asked to stand for that recognition.

A unison prayer may be included for the congregation. Such a prayer may be like the following:

> Lord God, whose work at creation testifies to thine artistry, and whose gifts to us in creation demonstrates thy benevolence, receive our thanksgiving today. We praise Thee that Thou hast called us to our work, and we ask Thee to honor the efforts we make in Thy name. We offer thanks for all those who serve us and make creation good. We thank Thee for those who even at this moment work that we might be free to worship and rest. And now, O God, we celebrate with these who have completed a long period of their life's work; we rejoice with them in the vocation which lies ahead. As they have blessed us in their careers, so we ask Thee that they may bless us in all they choose to do in these good years. Renew in each of us day by day an abiding consciousness of Thy call and direction that we may serve Thee, and Thy Son Jesus Christ.

Following worship, the retirees may be asked to stand at the altar area of the sanctuary to be greeted by all the church family. In larger churches, name tags will help those who may not know them all.

Such a worship emphasis will surely produce a significant level of consciousness about work and retirement far beyond the effort required to plan and carry out such a service. The acknowledgement and recognition of the retirees may open the door for some conversation with the pastor about ministry which can be done by these people in and through the established church program.

Worship, however, is only one aspect of rituals and programs associated with this passage from one stage of life to the next. Like every transition time, the individual leaves one life stage and goes into another; the person separates and then is incorporated into something else. The church can and should be involved not only in the transition in the worship ritual, but also in the rituals of leaving and joining.

The church can be involved in at least two ways prior to any recognition of retirement in a worship service. First, the church has a place in the preparation process. Not everyone talks openly about retirement plans, but I know of no retiree who did not spend hours and days and months poring over income figures to see if there would be enough money to live on. I doubt that anyone has ever retired without spending considerable time either thinking about or talking about what life would be like without going to work every day. Some handle these issues very well; others deal with them very poorly. One man confided in me several years after his retirement that he had more money during retirement than he ever had when he worked, yet he was always afraid the checks might stop or his savings would prove insufficient for his needs. Many others, on the other hand, retire and discover they have fewer financial resources than they need; this becomes a worrisome issue and takes much of the enjoyment from these otherwise good years. Management of both time and money always prove somewhat different after one leaves a career. The church can speak to these and other concerns, providing some forum for their discussion.

Somewhere within the church program, a multisession series or a one-evening workshop might be arranged. The leaders should be a pastor or teacher who can deal with the Christian vocation issue, an articulate and knowledgeable retiree with whom the group can identify, and an expert on the subject of senior adult living. If these leaders are not available in the local church, they may be found in other churches or through the denomination. The person who may best plan and organize such a program may be a senior adult

in the church. The pastor may help with the early organization, choosing the leaders and even suggesting those in the
church who might be invited by a letter or a card. But the
pastor need not be the one to carry the full responsibility for
the program. Smaller churches may want to join with other
churches in their communities and make the forum/work-
shop ecumenical. Local associations of churches are often
able to provide organizational skills, leadership, advertising,
and even funds to make such a program more effective than
might be possible by a single church.

A second possible means of involvement by the church,
prior to any recognition of the retiree in a worship service
may be the presence of the pastor or a representative of the
church in any formal ceremony given by the employer. Pastors are occasionally invited to such dinners or ceremonies/
receptions; if they know in advance of such plans, they may
even ask to share in them. When the church is represented,
the symbolic message says that work and retirement are
important to God—and this person in transition deserves,
needs, and probably wants the involvement of the faith community. These occasions should provide an opportunity to
look back without apology and recount something of the
individual's faithfulness and accomplishments.

Unfortunately, many of these ceremonies of retirement
tend to shortchange such summaries, gloss over the pain of
leaving, and hurry to the cliches about a life of perpetual
leisure. A caring and sensitive pastor can be there to talk
with the retiree and his/her family about the ambivalence
between memory and planning, between sadness and excitement, between pride and anxiety. The representative of God
is there to ask good questions about what the person remem-
bers most, did best, and wants to be remembered for. Beyond
asking the right questions and listening, the pastor is a symbolic presence whose importance cannot be overestimated.

When these ceremonies of leaving have ended and the ritual recognitions are done, the person enters retirement. The best anyone can hope for is for that retirement will be another vocation. For most retirees, the pace, the schedule, and the activities will be scaled down from the years on the job. Yet, such scaling down need not become inactivity. The church may prove to be an invaluable resource in deciding what groups to join, what responsibilities to accept, what directions to take. If the church has been involved in the planning stage prior to retirement, and offered ritual recognition in the context of worship, the church will have earned a hearing during the early period of retirement.

Whenever possible, the new retiree should be approached by someone in church leadership who will ask, "What would you like to do? What can we help you become a part of?" Of course, the stock answer usually comes back that the person wants to do nothing or the person wants some time to find out how much time and how many commitments are already established. After a year of trying out golf clubs, fishing tackle, and camping equipment, the new sewing machine or gardening equipment, some of these people will take on part-time employment, regular volunteer work, or some major project in the church. Along the way, some of them will want a pastor or church leader to talk with about the options.

I remember well the man who retired from an administrative position and vowed never again to do anything else in administration; he took such a job in his church, performed it beautifully, and seemed to enjoy it thoroughly. I know a man who promised himself he would not sit at home or be forever in his wife's way; he took several volunteer positions in the community and the church and makes a noticable difference to many people. I think of several people who tell me regularly as I pass them in the church buildings or see them after worship. "Let me know if you need help with anything." Retirement entered well and lived best may be the most giving time of one's life. The church can help these years to be so.

Most churches are fueled by the energy, time, and commitment of senior adults. These volunteers work in the church offices, care for the property, provide transportation, oversee building projects, arrange flowers, manage the libraries, lead committees and boards, and do the hundreds of onstage or behind-the-scenes tasks necessary for the church to function as an institution. All of them want very much to be needed, to be associated with institutions and issues that matter, and to be appreciated. They want the same things as when they worked in their jobs before retirement.

If the period of time immediately following the retirement ceremonies requires incorporation into the new life-style, the church is an excellent incorporator. Senior adults already settled into retirement can provide the best help in the incorporation process. Sunday school classes, men's groups, women's organizations, and seniors' organizations offer the warmest of welcome for these new retirees. Many of the larger churches have very large and active groups which travel, meet weekly for lunch and programs, and conduct many of the ministries of their churches. Participants are given an opportunity to be involved at whatever level they choose. Sometimes, involvement in these organizations opens many other doors for explorations into various activities and ministries. But whichever organizations and leaders reach out to newly retired people may not be as important as just being certain someone does reach out.

Of all the transitions from one life stage to the next, retirement may be the most neglected by society in general and the church in particular. With the increasing number of retirees, however, and in light of generally longer and healthier lifespans, the church is beginning to recognize the importance of her role in the transition between the working years and retirement.

Notes

1. Studs Terkel, *Working* (New York: Partheon Books, 1974).

2. D. Elton Trueblood, *The Common Ventures of Life* (New York: Harper and Row Publishers, 1949).

3. D. Elton Trueblood, *Your Other Vocation* (New York: Harper and Row Publishers, 1952).

6
Death

"I have finished my course" (1 Tim. 4:7, KJV).

I could assign a dozen names to the story line which never changes very much. A routine pastoral call to a member of the church no longer able to attend worship, an office appointment with an elderly member who may never have been in my study before, a home visit at the request of an aging church member. We may get right to the issue; we may share small talk as I await the real reason for the visit. The lady in her mid-to-late seventies says, "My children won't talk to me about this." Or she says, "Every time I bring up this subject to my children or friends, they tell me I have plenty of time to think about it; that I shouldn't worry about it now."

Then I ask, although I know the answer because I have heard it many times before, "What would you like to talk about?" We then spend our visit in discussion about a funeral, pallbearers, Scripture lessons, music, flowers, burial, and memorials. Sometimes the person will discuss what should be done about life-support systems in the event health has deteriorated and no hope remains. If she is like most of those who want to talk to family members, friends, and pastors, she already has much of her planning done in writing. Her preparation is part of her death rituals, and her carefulness indicates the importance of everything she has done; she is summing up her life and arranging her legacy. In many ways what she does is a gift to those closest to her. She is doing the planning and preparation others would be required to do if she were less careful.

The matter-of-factness of her voice further suggests the absence of fear. Like many great, famous, and heroic models of history, this senior adult assesses the days remaining in light of the days past and sees death and dying as a part of the entire fabric.

Unfortunately, the reluctance of well-meaning members of the nuclear and extended family to enter such discussions and planning may be tantamount to rejecting a wonderful gift, bypassing invaluable lessons. What may seem like a concern to protect someone they love from worry about dying is probably their own effort to protect themselves from anticipatory grief. Nevertheless, these senior adults have been through all the passages in the life cycle. They have presided over most of them in the development of their own children and have grown in the depth of meaning in their own personal transitions. Whether they choose to verbalize their understanding of both passages and rituals connected with such transitions, this senior generation has been there and they have seen it all. In all cases, their chosen rituals connected with the final passage of their lives are significant not only for them but for everyone they will leave behind.

Surely, the intensity of feelings and the care with which one's death is discussed underline this ultimate passage. For those in the prime of life, death looms as the last enemy and the one most to be avoided. For one who has passed from one life stage to the next and the next and the next, death may not be so frightening. Even when dying poses great threat, those in their latter years would like to be able to face it well-prepared and thoroughly supported. For those who will be left, as well as the one who will die, the care and the appropriateness of the rituals may mean substantial difference in the levels of fear and grief. In most cases, grief begins for everyone well before death comes. The early rituals help deal with everybody's grief.

Like the other rites of passage, death really includes separation, transition, and incorporation. Every culture has its set and well-defined patterns associated with the passage from life through death. Within our culture and among the various ethnic groups and religious faiths, patterns may vary. Even so, a certain uniformity exists and binds all our people together. For every major transition, religious faith provides the rituals and the interpretations which enable us to navigate such powerful and threatening passages. The church, for even the most peripheral Christians, serves as keeper of the rituals, administrator of the customs.

A Look at the Customs

Like the other passages, we tend to pay the greatest attention to the transition rituals—in this case, the funeral service and the burial. What goes on before and after the formal services, however, are rituals and are more carefully arranged and observed than we may initially recognize.

Prior to Death

Many years before most of us die, we begin to make plans. The last will and testament serves to initiate the process of preparation. Sometimes the birth of a child causes a couple to be connected with the possibility that one of them may die. Who will care for the baby? Will there be enough money to meet the child's needs? What will happen to family possessions? If no will has been prepared by the time couples or individuals reach middle age, they are sometimes spurred into action by the untimely death of a friend or acquaintance their own age. Attorneys often see an increase in the number of clients who want to draw up a will after the death of a prominent young adult in the community. Other factors may be the death of one's own parents, international travel, or the onset of a health problem.

The will enables us to look specifically at the reality of death, its inevitability, and the control we can exercise even after we are gone. Even though the contents may change many times through the years, the basic document enables us to inventory our material possessions, our religious faith, and our relationships. This in itself is a ritual of major significance. Furthermore, such an exercise, while somber and private, offers us an opportunity to discuss our values and dreams with a few other people. Those whom we want to name as executors, guardians for our children, and officials for our funeral services need to be contacted for their permission; such communication opens doors for dealing with life's greatest issues, in conjunction with persons most important to us. These discussions ought never to be trivialized by any of the people approached, even if such issues threaten us as subjects we prefer not to face.

Another preparatory ritual is that consultation with the minister. Senior adults are seldom reluctant to discuss such issues with their ministers; younger adults often are extremely reluctant. Even when diagnosed with a terminal illness, those who are "not old" will tell their ministers, "Don't come and see me right now; I want my life to be as normal as possible until I can no longer have it that way." But when such discussions are established and conducted over a period of time, the benefits for persons in any age group are enormous. Great theological/spiritual issues can be explored—the meaning of life and death, personal worth, work and vocation, relationships, family, personal achievements, failures and regrets. Most of all, a deep relationship between pastor and parishioner can develop, serving to strengthen the faith of both persons. As a result, expressions of gratitude and confession, affirmations of faith, and deepening of spiritual life often emerge.

Of course, similar discussions with family members and close friends include all the issues discussed with the clergy and attorneys; these discussions also seek to assign responsibility for carrying out the person's wishes, as well as soliciting affirmation that such decisions are good, right, and appropriate.

I recall a hospital visit in which many of these elements of preparation came into play. A prominent man in the church and community sent for his two ministers/friends. We went, not sure what the issues would be. He sent his family from the room and asked us to close the door. He reviewed carefully the plans he had made for his death, his finances, his funeral. When he had recited what he had obviously rehearsed, he said, "I called you here together because I want to know if you think what I have done is right." He was asking for spiritual input from two clergymen he respected. Together, the three of us had participated in one of those major rituals of preparation. This visit would serve to make the actual transition period less difficult for everyone concerned. The more carefully and thoroughly these preparation rituals are carried out, the better prepared everyone will be when death actually comes—and the more potentially celebrative the transition rituals can be.

At the Time of Death

The moment of death often lasts for days. The person lingers, either unconscious or in varying degrees of pain and discomfort. Every breath seems to be the last. Family and friends gather, come and go, remember, and make plans. These are days in which the church may be able to move in and out of the setting, offering quiet expressions of concern. Close friends in the Christian community often take turns sitting, nursing, and providing household assistance. Some appear at the home with food. Others stop by the house or hospital room with pledges of prayers and expressions of love. These are a part of the cultural rituals which provide visible and tangible evidence of a larger but intimate community.

The minister remains for the dying person and the family the most visible symbol of God's presence. If the pastor has been in careful communication during confinement and illness, ministry simply extends itself in a more intense manner at the moment of death. If I know in advance of a person's deteriorating health and impending death, I ask the family to call me at any time they need me, and especially as soon as death occurs. When I am called, if I can arrive soon enough, I try to offer appropriate Scriptures and prayers at the bedside. In the hospital, the nursing staff nearly always assists in providing privacy; they postpone many of the essential duties of their office so the proper spiritual rites can be performed. If the hospital staff happens to be insensitive to these needs—and they seldom are—I ask for the time and the privacy to be alone with the family.

Because ministers are more familiar with customs and logistics at such a difficult time, the family may ask for practical direction: what funeral home, who telephones, when to meet for planning the services. Some ministers offer to participate in the planning at the funeral home: selection of casket, wording of obituary, setting of time and place for the funeral, and arrangement of visitation. Many of these practical matters involve theological issues, especially as they reflect the quality of the person's life and bear witness to the Christian hope. The minister's involvement in these practical matters will facilitate pastoral care later because, during the planning process, the family will often express pain, guilt, regret, fear, and a sense of damaged relationships.

When the time comes to plan the actual funeral service, the minister should insist upon a quiet and private place with as many of the family members present as possible. Such a setting provides opportunity for extensive sharing about the life of the one who has died and his/her influence upon those planning the service. Members of the family might relate personal stories and recollections about the person; such reflections become a part of the healing process and provide both family members and the minister with deeper insight into the feelings of those most affected by the death. This kind of participation enables everyone involved to become part of the caring and healing network. These are times of expression of grief as well as affirmations of the noble dimensions of life itself.

During such a meeting, the pastor has an opportunity to interpret the funeral service as a time of worship—including praise and thanksgiving, the celebration of life, the affirmation of our humanity, and the reality of eternal life. This can be done without extended explanations or even the impression that the minister is preaching to the family. Family members frequently use this setting as an opportunity to ask questions, express doubts and fears, or give vent to some of their own frustrations and even relational difficulties.

In the course of the planning, favorite Scriptures, poems, and music come to light. Some selections will be more appropriate and helpful than others. To this day I cringe to remember some of the things I have been asked to read in the service; I shudder to recall some of the music I have heard at funerals. But my overall experience suggests that families really respect the judgment of their pastors and can be guided to what is best and appropriate. Very often they will say, "You know better than we do what should be included."

Nevertheless, they are grateful to be asked for suggestions, and frequently their suggestions are helpful. If I have a clear sense of the service as these conversations unfold, I will read several scriptural texts to them and we will discuss their significance. The ministry of the Word can begin to take place immediately.

The Funeral Service

The central ritual is, of course, the funeral service itself. In most cases, I prefer the service to be conducted at the church rather than at the funeral home. This seems to be especially important for those whose lives have been deeply invested in the church. When the service is in the sanctuary, the possibilities for worship are greatly increased. Hymns may be used; responsive Scripture lessons can be included; members of the church can be a part of the service as musicians, ushers, and even worship leaders. The sanctuary as a familiar place suggests participation and I find that most families want the congregation to be involved. In the church I serve, such a practice has been so long-standing that when a funeral is planned for the sanctuary, the family and the congregation expect to participate.

Too little has been said about congregational involvement in worship in general, and in the rites of passage in particular. In too many of the churches in the free-church tradition the congregation is an audience—listening, watching, but involving themselves only in silent ways. Yet, in the matter of funerals, a death has touched everyone present. The rituals belong to the faith community as well as to the family most intimately affected. The lessons from Scripture, the prayers, and the hymns belong to the gathered community; their voices as well as their hearts and minds are needed. These audible, unified expressions of faith bear witness to power and strength of both faith and hope. Carlyle Marney, a noted

Baptist pastor, often told his listeners, "No man is spectator to his own salvation."

What kind of ritual funeral/memorial service is planned in conjunction with the family of the one who has died, and conducted with participation of the gathered faith community? Here is such a service in outline form, offered as a kind of model. I am fully aware that there are as many variations as churches and ministers, most of them significant and viable, some of them more powerful and creative than this model.

I usually meet with the family in a room near the sanctuary about ten minutes prior to the service. I introduce myself because some from out of town may not know me, and I express on behalf of the church both welcome and condolences. I talk briefly about the service itself and the logistics of entering and leaving the sanctuary. If an order of service is printed, copies are distributed. I offer a prayer specifically for the family.

When we have entered as a group and the prelude of organ music has ended, the service moves with some variations as follows:

> *Call to Worship* (Ps. 46; John 11:25-26; Matt. 11:28-30, or another)

> *Prayer of Invocation*
> Almighty God, in whom we live and move and have our being, receive our worship on the occasion of the death of our loved one, (full name), and grant us both comfort and assurance of Thy mercy. We beg Thee, O God, use every expression of ministry by Thy people to remind those whose grief is so severe that Thou art good and just in all Thy ways. Receive our prayers and hymns, and all our words of praise, as expressions of our love

for Thee and one another, in the name of Him who for our sakes has overcome sin and death, even our Lord Jesus Christ. Amen (The Lord's Prayer may be spoken by the congregation here, after the Prayer of Consolation, or at the place of burial.)

Hymn of Praise

Lesson from the Scriptures

(May be a responsive psalm or other Scripture of praise.)

Anthem, Solo, or Choral Music

Scriptures of Consolation and Hope

(A series of Scripture selections either chosen to follow a single motif, provide consolation, or the text for the sermon.)

Sermon

Prayer of Consolation

Merciful Father, we acknowledge to Thee and to one another the pain we feel in the loss of our brother/sister, (Name). To remember all he/she has given to us fills us with gratitude, but sharpens our sense of loss. Grant us day by day to be surrounded by the influences of his/her life, and supported in our loss by those who also grieve and thereby understand. Enable us to take up every righteous concern, every gift of the Spirit, every noble quality of his/her life, and carry them forward as a fitting memorial. For (names of nuclear family) we ask special warmth and strength of thy Spirit and of thy church, that in time, their grief may turn fully to gratitude, and that their pain shall turn to the joy of those whose lives have been transformed by the love of another. Hear us and help us through Jesus Christ, who Himself experienced all the pain of death and sorrow until He was fully united with Thee. Amen

Hymn of Affirmation

Benediction (May be omitted if continuity between the sanctuary service and graveside service is to be maintained.)

If the service is conducted at the funeral home, unison prayers, congregational hymns, and responsive readings may be difficult to arrange. Even in churches where secretarial help is available, the time of death and the kinds of arrangements may make a printed bulletin impossible. Few funeral homes have hymnals. However, if resources are available, and a bulletin can be printed, some congregational participation can be included by printing those prayers and readings they will share. I continue to maintain that every effort to involve the people is more than worthwhile.

The graveside service should be understood as a continuation of the service at the church or the funeral home. Instead of another ritual, the care of the body actually expresses faith in the God's order of things. The format I have felt most comfortable with is offered as a model; Yet, I am conscious of others equally significant.

Scripture Lesson   (Ps. 23; 1 Cor. 15:50-58; 1 Thess. 4:13-18; or one of several others)
Committal (using Genesis 3:19 or another such appropriate text. Earth may be sprinkled over the casket.)

Prayer of Committal
Almighty God, thou who hast created all living beings and ordained the cycles of life itself, we return to the earth the body of thy servant, (*Name*). We rejoice that the spirit lives on, and we are sustained by the promise of our Lord Jesus Christ, that where He is, there shall be all those who love Him. Keep us all in this hope, for we also live in anticipation of our own deaths. Grant us

to reach out one to one another for comfort, love, and support, growing in Thy grace. Maintain in our memories the influences and the gifts of him/her whose life we honor this day. Uphold us always as we pray the prayer of our Lord.

The Lord's Prayer (If not prayed earlier.)
Benediction

After the Funeral Service

The rites of this passage do not end with the burial of the body. With or without the church, family members closest to the person who died will conduct additional memorial rituals. Regular visits to the cemetery, memorial contributions to various charities, and in some cases memorial announcements in newspapers at birthday or death anniversaries all suggest ongoing rituals. How do these fit into the "preparation, transition, incorporation" triad suggested earlier?

Incorporation must be seen in the rituals of death as inclusion of the person into some acceptable realm of memory. The church speaks of resurrection and life after death as incorporation into the "great cloud of witnesses"; those of us yet alive, however, are unable to receive them into a realm we do not occupy. We tend to deal with this limitation by making them a part of our memory, and committing them by faith to a world we can only surmise. Both require additional rituals.

I suggest three rituals as means by which grieving families complete their involvement in their loved ones' passage from life into death. The first of these will obviously be direct pastoral care—the continuation of the church involved in the passage. The pastor is most professionally involved, particularly in the care of the intimate details of grief and recovery. I follow a procedure which provides me with structure and continuity in this care. My secretary keeps track of dates; she places on my desk one-month, three-months, six-months, and one-year reminders of each death date. In one way or another, not always with a visit or a conference, I will check on the progress of the family members with whom I am most involved.

The most important contact for me is always arranged within ten days of the funeral service. I take a copy of a little book about the grief process as a gift to the family.[1] This serves as an outline for my grief work with them. Whom I see in the family and how often I see them depends upon their needs—and my own ability to assess those needs.

In the process of my own attempts at pastoral care, I am always keenly aware of the involvement of others in the church. Someone has telephoned. Another has visited. A family has included the grieving person in a dinner party or an outing. These church members often let me know what is happening and call me when they think I can be helpful. They help me assess the need for my own involvement. The weeks and months after a death require a broad-based network of pastoral care, including both pastor and people. Such a process is a part of the rites of passage at death.

Another of those rituals particularly important to the congregation I serve, is a "Book of Memorials." Many years ago, the pastor before me led the congregation to establish a system for memorial gifts to the church. A book was put inside the vestibule table. In the book are inscribed memorial contributions—who contributed and in whose name. Each Sunday the book is opened to a different page. Each memorial is duly noted in the church newsletter as well. Such a ritual helps the church keep alive the memory of those whose lives have been integral to the life of the church; they also help the family realize a measure of the support they are being given in their efforts to affirm life in the face of death. Through the memorial program, the church has received many tangible expressions of sympathy and respect; these exist as constant and positive reminders to members of the person's family.

A third, after-the-funeral ritual is a memorial service conducted every spring. Each Memorial Day weekend, on the Sunday before the holiday, the worship service is devoted to remembering and honoring those of our fellowship who died in the previous twelve months. All Saints Day on the liturgical calendar is the more commonly used date, but November proved to be inconvenient in the worship schedule in our church. The national holiday, however, has proven a very effective occasion.

Hymns, anthems, lessons, and prayers are chosen to support the memorial theme. The liturgy is designed to offer a measure of both memory and affirmation. The high point of the service focuses on a small styrofoam cross placed on the altar table. The cross is covered with live greenery. Each name of those who have died is read from the printed order of worship, the chairperson of the memorials committee places a white carnation in the cross, and the organist strikes one chime. When all the names have been read, the congregation joins in a unison prayer of thanksgiving for the lives of those we have remembered, including intercession for those whose grief and loss have not yet been resolved.

The value of such a memorial service extends far beyond its ministry to those who are yet experiencing grief. In the words of John Donne, the bell really tolls for each one of us. We have all lost loved ones. We will each one day be numbered among the dead. Mortality, loss, and grief are part of the human condition. Whenever and wherever they are marked, the participants are legion.

Customs in Transition

Our culture in general and the church in particular are undergoing serious changes in the rituals associated with death and dying. Like all best-of-times, worst-of-times transitions, the news is both good and bad. Danger times are also opportunity times.

The bad news may be the lessening of involvement by the membership of the local churches. As our mobile society has uprooted us from our places of birth and families of origin, so it has set in perpetual motion the membership of local churches. Many of our members work in distant places, or in jobs which do not allow time away for funerals of nonrelatives. More women are employed. Many of our church members have not grown up in the community and may not be well-known at the time of their death. The result of these changes taken as a whole is often sparsely attended funeral services. Many who die are separated by great distance from family and one-time close friends; many who would like to participate in the rituals are unable to do so. All this means that local churches will need to pay much closer attention to funeral services, enlisting all who are able and available to be present as representatives of the larger church family. The criteria for attending a funeral may no longer be family or close friendship.

The good news of these radical transitions may be the reemergence of a sense of the importance of ritual at the time of death, at least in the consciousness of greater numbers of people in the church. Much more is being said about death and dying. Television, periodicals, and films seem to be dealing more in depth with the emotions and spiritual needs in this transition time. The hospice movement is providing people with greater flexibility about dying at home; a broader representation of professionals is being made available to families in which a member faces death. More open discussion about rituals before, during, and following death will mean an increase in support for everyone. These elements can influence the quality of the rituals surrounding death; the church can make these influences even more positive than they might be otherwise.

One quality in the best of rituals will never grow obsolete or change, however. That quality is sensitivity, or compassion which seems to be its companion. Ritual without compassion and sensitivity makes transitions worse, not better. When the faith community feels deeply, cares intensely, and shares unselfishly at the time of death, the support level enables a dignified death. Such infused ritual provides order in what may otherwise be chaos. And that order follows those who are left until they can again sing and laugh and be glad.

Note

1. Granger E. Westberg, *Good Grief* (Philadelphia: Fortress Press, 1971).

7

Transitions in Marriage, Residence, and Career

"Perfect love casts out fear" (1 John 4:18).

The essential rites of passage—birth, marriage, and death —vary from culture to culture and even within a given society. In some expressions of faith in our own culture, birth and baptism/circumcision are joined as part of the same passage. Among others of us, birth and baptism are distinct transitions and require separate rituals. In some cultures, puberty rites and marriage are joined; in our own culture, the passage from childhood to adulthood is much less clearly defined; marriage may or may not be a part of that transition.

Further, some rites of passage become part of a given culture almost by necessity. Our culture has added a rite of graduation; retirement rites are in the process of taking shape and in the next century may be as important as graduation. Because civilization is dynamic rather than static, the rites of passage—what we do and when—must change to express what happens to us as individuals within context of tribe or clan. Because the church serves as primary guardian of the rites of passage, especially for those in any way identified with Christianity, the church has a role in adjusting existing rituals and adding others. As the church identifies powerful and significant changes, those affecting both individuals and the larger community, the church seeks to respond in appropriate ways. Adjusting and adding rituals stands as part of the stewardship of the church. Such changes will, of course, be endorsed or rejected by participation (or lack of participation) by the people. Such checks and balances are part of every social structure.

My own experience with dedication of babies serves as an example. Other ministers and churches could relate similar stories. The first baby dedication I conducted was in a morning worship service in 1970. Thereafter, the people began to ask if the next one had been scheduled. Their acceptance and desire to participate served as an initial endorsement; a larger numerical attendance on those days suggested further that we were addressing a perceived need. Who among us in the church can look well into the twenty-first century and know exactly what changes will take place in the rituals of transition over which we will preside?

Indeed, three such transitions in our culture have become so widespread and so powerful as to require consideration as passages needing rites. None of the three deserve the same level of attention as birth, baptism, marriage, and death; but then, neither do graduation and retirement. They are important enough, however, to merit consideration for some sort of lesser ritual observance. These are divorce, moving from one community to another, and career changes.

Divorce

The church has not handled divorce very well. On the one hand, we have preached grace, redemption, healing, and support by the faith community. On the other hand, we have taken sometimes harsh and judgmental positions toward the people involved in the dissolution of a marriage. At times it has appeared that the church would like to mediate the grace of healing to those broken by a failure in marriage, but we have proceeded with the caution that comes from not wanting to be misunderstood (that is, if we are too grace-full, we might be interpreted as being soft on divorce).

Some attack the church for being too judgmental, and others charge the church with being soft on divorce. Each have their ammunition. In a debate so evenly divided, we can be certain the issue has no easy solutions. No one who takes seriously the sanctity of marriage would deny the ideal of permanance, of a growing relationship, of the necessity for commitment and hard work. As long as the family assumes part of the task of guarding values and passing them along to each succeeding generation, permanance and commitment in marriage must be the norm. The church supports that standard as divinely ordained. The church must continue to do so.

People are not perfect, however, and neither are marriages. Some weddings never initiate marriage. Hardly any extended family is without a tale of a wedding that should never have taken place. Some marriages die; something of love and commitment existed early but could not be sustained in the changes or lack of changes in the lives of the couple. Some marriages are put to death by the sins of one or both of the couple. When people are broken, crippled, injured, and hurt, the church should seek to be present; when those damaged lives need a bridge to healing, the church ought to seek to be the bridge builder. When these bridges, passages, transitions require patterns worthy of being repeated, rituals are formed, used, and reused until they become rites of passage. Like those already established, they will consist of preparation, transition, and incorporation. Do any such rituals now exist? Can such rituals find a place in our worship?

To address the first question, consider the impact of a divorce court welfare officer in Birmingham, England. In 1980 Sheila Davis wrote a few "positive sentences" as a means to help reduce the "rancor and recrimination" of parents locked in child custody disputes. She asks such couples to join hands and say,

> "Goodbye [sic] and thank you for the good times we had in our marriage. I wish you all the best. Our relationship will continue as mother and father of our children, but not as husband and wife. Good luck."[1]

Obviously, Ms. Davis has not written a litany for Christian worship; she has suggested a need for a personal rather than a merely legal dissolution. As evidence of its value, she offers an important report: what she has been doing all these years has "caught on." We can only suspect the reason has something to do with the need for constructive closure, a good-bye which does not minimize pain but does avoid some of the destructiveness we usually associate with failure. What seems most important are face-to-face good-byes said by both persons.

I have not located such a litany to be incorporated in a public worship service. If one exists, I suspect it is seldom or never used. The rites of passage celebrated publicly all have a joyful and forward-looking tenor to them. Even death and funerals have that anticipation about them. In all but a few divorces, the pain of failure and sense of loss dominate the couple, the children, and the extended family to such a degree that no kind of "celebration" seems possible. Furthermore, emotional nakedness requires a level of privacy, even within a loving faith community. All this is to say that I doubt the wisdom or effectiveness of a "ceremony of divorce." I cannot envision or advocate very many couples standing before their church family repeating a litany dissolving their marriage.

This does not mean, however, that divorce should never be mentioned in worship, especially in a sympathetic way.

The prayers and sermons can address endings and beginnings, sin and redemption, pain and healing, failure and grace—and do so specifically in the context of discussions about marriage and divorce. *The* (1970 Presbyterian) *Worshipbook,* with many litanies and prayers, includes a prayer "For the Divorced or Separated."

> God of grace: you are always working to hold us together, to heal division, and make love strong. Help men and women whose marriages break up to know that you are faithful. Restore confidence, bring understanding, and ease the hurt of separation. If they marry others, instruct them in better love, so that vows may be said and kept with new resolve; through Jesus Christ our Lord. Amen.[2]

If a prayer the sole subject of which is divorce and separation is not used, the subject matter can and should be included as a part of other prayers, particularly on occasions of family emphases. Worship leaders may be surprised by the positive response of congregations to prayers for those divorced or separated.

To the second question, "Can such rituals find a place in our public worship?" I suspect the answer is that it is unlikely, especially as a formal and public rite of passage. I would very quickly add, however, that some formal and less public ritual may be needed and may find acceptance. The personality at the center of such a ritual would be the minister, perhaps functioning in cooperation with or as a pastoral counselor. This pastoral care giver often stands on the front line when the cracks in the relationship begin to show. The couple whose marriage is in trouble will usually approach the minister first.

In many cases the couple coming to see the pastor has already determined the outcome. The session enables one or both of them to say to parents and friends, "We did everything we could; we *even* went to see the minister." The implication is, of course, that not even God could save our marriage! The minister will, nevertheless, give the couple and their marriage every professional and spiritual wisdom possible, referring them to a more specialized counselor if possible. What is the role of the clergy, however, when all efforts to save the marriage fail?

My own experience has been that the couple, or at least one member of the couple withdraws from the minister and from the church. Perhaps guilt and/or shame are overwhelming. Sometimes a sense of rejection, even when the church wants to be inclusive, drives this person from the church. Failure on their part or a spirit of judgmentalism from church may also contribute to the alienation. For any or all of these reasons, the pastor remains throughout the process an important figure.

Can this Christian shepherd in a quiet, private way preside over the dissolution of a marriage in such a way that healing can be facilitated and eventual reincorporation take place? I believe so. I suggest that wherever possible, and as soon as the minister has a clear sense that the marriage is irreparable, he/she may assume the initiative and call the couple together. The three of them—or in some cases, the Christian counselor should be invited—can discuss some ritual of transition. A proposed ritual should be printed and discussed with the couple at this time. Later, at a mutually agreeable time, perhaps in the pastor's study or in the church sanctuary, a private service of dissolution may take place. With only the couple and one or two professionals, the children and/or other members of their extended families, a ritual of dissolution can be both healing and instructive.

The pastor may begin with a prayer invoking God's presence and acknowledging God's love. Romans 8:38-39 can be read to underscore the unconditional nature of God's love for all of us. The couple, reading from printed copies of the rite, may affirm in unison a mutual acknowledgement, agreement. The following serves as a model:

> I, John/Mary, give thanks to God for the love and the joy which have been present in this marriage. I pledge to keep sacred the memory of everything good and lovely we experienced together. I further acknowledge my own sins of word, thought, and deed which have contributed to this failure; I ask forgiveness of God, of you, (John/Mary), of our children, and family and friends. Finally, I promise in both attitude and in word to refrain from anything which may be hurtful to you, our families, and our friends. I pray God's leadership in our separate lives.

A prayer for God's mercy and assistance should follow at this point, either by the pastor or the pastoral counselor. If the ceremony is conducted in the sanctuary at the altar, a triple candle—the unity candle often used in wedding ceremonies—can be partially extinguished. The center candle can be put out by the couple holding a snuffer; the other two candles should be left burning.

Such a ceremony, as brief as it is, serves as a transition in which the church offers continued involvement in each of their lives. Each of them must be reincorporated into the faith community, and the way has been prepared for that reincorporation to take place. The minister and the pastoral counselor may continue to play a role in the adjustment period, even helping to negotiate painful and delicate pathways. The involvement of the minister in such a ritual as this makes such a future role possible.

Has the time come for such a ritual? Those churches

which are part of the free-church tradition have an opportunity to test the waters.

Moving Away

Another transition in our culture, and one which may require some formal Christian ritual, occurs when a family or individual moves from our community and the local church. After all, we are a society on the move, and it happens often. Major corporations keep moving van companies in the black. Fulfillment of the American dream, always just around the next bend, makes us more than willing to accept a job transfer. But the price is high. We are separated from our family roots and distant friendships are difficult to maintain. Even though we move around a great deal, the separations seem to get more difficult rather than easier. The church provides some stability; we might provide some additional support if we worked as hard at saying good-bye as we do at saying hello.

Church newsletters reveal a great deal about the mentality and spirituality of the local church and local churches. This is especially true of good-byes. I am intrigued by the newsletter section entitled, ". . . and the Lord added." Some churches assign numbers to new members. Other churches list the deacon responsible for the "addition." A worthy effort to announce a new arrival and ensure incorporation into the fellowship! But I have never seen a newsletter with a section entitled, ". . . and the Lord took away." Facetious? Not entirely. Members leave churches. Some become offended and stop attending; others go to the church down the road. They leave in pain and we let them go in silence. Perhaps we have no other choice. But what about those who move to another place far away?

I remember vividly a lesson from my family's last move—the only move our two daughters had experienced. We knew it would be difficult for them, and it was. Our younger daughter was six years old at the time. We knew about the move several months in advance and worked hard to prepare the children. We assumed the little one was handling it all very well, even though she had said very little. One day she blurted out three questions—almost in the same breath. "Why are we moving? The people will think we don't like them anymore! Will the movers scratch the furniture? Do we have to put all those boxes out?" She was dealing with three elements present for everybody in every move: rejection, pain, and inventory!

Moving from one community to another involves the same process as the primary rites of passage: we leave something (separation); we experience a transition process; we are incorporated into a new setting/environment. Moving involves good-byes, a long ride, and a welcome. Most moves are so intense and include so much work and change, we hardly remember them when they have passed because we go through them in a state of shock! Unfortunately, unresolved grief never just disappears; it tends to go underground only to multiply and resurface, often inappropriately, much later. One of the roles of the church is that of guide, especially in the more painful of our transitions. The model must always be the way Jesus attended to His own disciples as He prepared to leave them. The Communion of the Lord's Supper attests to the effectiveness of His grief ministry. Each time the church gathers to celebrate Communion, we remember what happened, celebrate His spiritual presence, and anticipate reunion. Are not all these elements present in our earthly farewells?

Unfortunately, the church tends to sweep good-byes under the carpet. When our members announce they plan to move, we notice they begin to pull back in attendance, in the place where they usually sit in worship, in their conversation. Be-

cause the church does not always know how to say good-bye,
we allow this unsupported pulling back. The fact that our
newsletters say so little about those who leave may indicate
how poorly the church helps in this transition. But we can
do better.

The fellowship I serve has been struggling with all the rites
of passage for a long time. We are attempting to pay more
careful attention to the transition times through appropriate
rituals. We are learning together about good-byes of all
kinds. Three traditions seem to be emerging.

First, we are attempting to face honestly the pain of saying
good-bye. I recall two interviews which brought front and
center our need to do so. The first was with a young mother,
a Sunday School teacher, who came to tell me she was leaving the church. The church was not meeting her needs; she
was not comfortable with what she perceived to be our direction. She was not sure she would remain a Baptist, but she
planned to "look around." She expressed pain in separation;
I expressed pain in the sense that I felt we may have failed
her. In the end, I thanked her for the "exit interview" in
which we had both learned a great deal.

The other interview never took place. A family left the
church, looking for some magical solution to their personal
problems. I knew they would not find a miracle cure and the
years have verified my initial evaluation. But I wrote them
a letter and offered to meet with them to say good-bye and
offer my assistance in the transition. I never heard from
them, not because they were angry, but because they were
hurt and ashamed, and suspected leaving would not solve
their problems.

In both cases I saw the need for such a meeting. Whether
a person/family moves across town or across the nation,
appropriate farewells are important for everybody. Since
such interviews cannot take place between those leaving and

the entire congregation, someone in a leadership role must represent the church. Obviously the pastor cannot be involved in all of these, but a member of the membership committee or the deacon group could do so.

A second effort we are making—this one in worship—is a simple farewell at the conclusion of the last worship service the person(s) attends. We ask them ahead of time to allow us to call them to the altar area where I bid them farewell in behalf of the church. The benediction to worship includes a benediction upon them as well. The congregation then files by with their personal "Godspeeds."

A third means of ritualizing this passage is the notice of their new address in our weekly newsletter. Some of our people write cards of encouragement, expressing appreciation for them and their time in our midst.

Only one of these efforts—the formal farewell in the worship service can appropriately be called a formal ritual. Yet, the attempt at being involved in the lives of the people who are moving are all a part of a larger set of rites of passage from one place to another.

One word of caution seems in order. What is said in worship service and in the interview should be chosen carefully. Their leaving is not the end of the world; in fact, they are going to something, perhaps exciting, surely challenging. Some open recognition of grief ought to be present; overstated gloom or despair are inappropriate and will not contribute anything positive to the transition.

If possible within six months after the person or family moves, the church might write to express some interest in them, and especially inquire about their progress in locating a new church home. The rite of passage is not complete until the person or family is incorporated into a new setting.

Choice or Change of Career

During the middle years of the twentieth century, the church preached and taught a great deal about vocation—the idea that God "calls" men and women to their life's work. The church said that religious professionals are not the only ones to whom God speaks and whose choice of work God influences. Nonecclesiastical professionals, crafts people, and even laborers can experience a sense of the divine Voice in choosing their careers and in performing their "ministries" in the workplace. Nevertheless, little or no worship emphasis was given to acknowledging the actual "call" and/or accepting the call, except in the case of persons declaring for the professional ministry. Few if any ceremonies of dedication or commissioning underscored the "doctrine" of Christian vocation. Perhaps therein lies part of the current lack of emphasis upon the call of God to a person's "secular" life's work.

Has the church changed her mind about the doctrine of vocation? Probably not. Yet, the number and relative intensity of other doctrines and rituals which demand the attention of the church has meant we have been forced to put aside these and other such issues which also deserve attention. Both vocational choice and change of vocation have been deemphasized in the heat of many more demanding, intense and community-involved transitions. Even so, the church may look at her own lack of involvement in vocational issues in the latter part of this century. We may ask whether the absence of rituals during those years when we emphasized Christian vocation, as well as our recent silence about the doctrine of vocation itself, have not at least contributed to some of our society's vocational uncertainties.

A case in point has been the well-documented struggles of young adults in their twenties to settle into careers. Much has been written about young people drifting from job to job, moving back home with their parents, starting and stopping graduate programs, spending years in counseling, and generally feeling the frustration of not knowing what they want. I have alluded earlier to the same lack of direction, calling, and altruism often seen even in seminary students, those whom we would expect to be among our most surefooted young adults. Yet, far too many of them leave seminary terribly uncertain of their direction and openly admitting they are not at all sure of their calling.

Some of the brightest young adults I know tell me regularly they are "looking around"—that is, circulating resumes—even though they have been in their present positions only one year or so. Whether in secular or sacred careers, this unsettled segment of society should cause the church to look at what we are not saying and doing about the issue of vocation. Indeed, we can and should do more without trying to assume total responsibility for the developmental difficulties of young adults.

Another case in point is the changing role of women in our society. Increasing numbers of young women are choosing to pursue careers either along with marriage and homemaking or instead of that more traditional choice. Many other women, after their children attain some degree of independence, choose to return to school and/or enter the job market. Whether these women simply trade some of their homemaking energies and skills for secular careers, or answer the call of God to a vocation outside the home, they, too, need the ministry of the church. For them, some recognition of their passages, and the blessing of the faith community may be the most important gift the church has for them at that time.

If the unsettled nature of many young adults signals a need for the church's involvement, and if the changing roles of women call for our encouragement, the vast numbers of all those who struggle with any career change also need the faith community. Those who announce their career intentions, go through the preparation process, work for a time in those careers, may not find leaving them acceptable to their families and friends. A twenty-eight-year-old minister resigned the church to which he had been pastor for four years and became a military chaplain. He told a friend, "The folks back home think I've left the ministry." When a middle-age physician left his practice for an administrative position in a health-care organization; his mother asked him if he didn't want to be a doctor anymore. A thirty-year-old school-teacher took a position with a large industrial corporation; she reported all sorts of negative reactions by her family and friends. Career changes often prove to be difficult, painful, costly, and even lonely. The church in pastoral care and in worship can lend support, encouragement, and even direction to those who have made such difficult decisions.

Preaching and worship provide both setting and content in bringing life transition into focus and then in supporting their resolution. Vocational transitions, like all passages, begin in the preparation process. Sermons, lessons, prayers and the offertory provide an overall theology of vocation. Each worship emphasis upon life as a trust and abilities as part of our stewardship help underscore the importance of our work. Pastors need not preach entire sermons devoted to the choice of a career; a single point in a sermon, or one paragraph or illustration can suggest the choice of career as a partnership with God. Introductions to the offertory naturally deal with stewardship, often with our participation in the ongoing work of creation. Prayers can and should try to speak about the various struggles of the congregation; one such struggle will always be with careers and vocations. Scripture lessons can be chosen to speak to the people about the call of God, about the stewardship of life, and about spiritual gifts to be used in every avenue of life.

One sentence in a prayer or a sermon can touch a chord in a worshiper and lead that person to discuss openly with the pastor or a friend issues which had been previously silent. The faith community can be available and involved in these deliberations. Of course the clergy often become involved in such consultations, but many wise and experienced laypersons can offer direction and support in the explorations as well.

Preaching and worship also provide encouragement and support during the transition. Sermons, prayers, and Scripture lessons—one sentence or one paragraph—can speak powerfully to those interviewing for new jobs, going back to school, saying good-bye to careers, or starting that new career. In any given worship service, someone will be standing at that transition point or walking through the passageway. For that person to know by a sentence in a sermon or a prayer or a Scripture reading that the minister and/or the congregation is sensitive to that tension is itself a powerful ritual of support. Passages are seldom easy; if some ritual, no matter how small, blesses the transition, leaving and arriving are made less traumatic and even more significant.

Two particular Sundays in the church year offer opportunities to address vocational issues: the Sunday nearest to Labor Day, and the Sunday nearest to local high-school graduations. Even if these worship services are not completely devoted to themes related to work, careers, achievement, or life goals, the issue of vocation may be included in parts of the worship service.

The actual transitions can be noted in the church newsletter if such a section is customarily reserved for news of the church family. Even if no public mention is made of individual vocational beginnings or changes, a major part of any church's pastoral care includes personal recognitions by the professional staff and leaders. I am always a bit surprised by the grateful response I receive to a handwritten note to a person who has just passed through such a transition as a job change, promotion, or award.

Reevaluation

Human beings and our societies seem always to be involved in transitions. We are ever preparing for some change, going through some passage or another, and being incorporated into our new situations. Because the church is part of the very societies to which we minister, the church is also dynamic and changing. None of the rites of passage over which we preside are prescribed in heaven and written in stone. Those rituals change over long periods of time according to the needs of people.

The leadership of local churches will maintain a healthy and dynamic set of rituals of passage if they maintain healthy pastoral contact with what is happening in the lives of the faith community. The issue is really how the household of faith can journey with those in transition, and contribute to the progress of the journey. Such ought always be part of the discussion among the leadership of every local church.

Notes

1. Lloyd Shearer, "Intelligence Report," *Parade,* May 28, 1988, p. 10.
2. *The Worshipbook* (Philadelphia: The Westminster Press, 1970), p.186.